Praise for *The*

"A lyric, hip-hop epic that n̶...̶
through its textures and its talismans — headlines,
beats, back-in-the-day vernacular."

—*Los Angeles Times*

"A beautifully written, loving portrait of a strong father
bringing his sons to manhood."

—*Booklist* (starred review)

"Coates brings the struggle of the streets to the page in language, verging on poetic, that is brutal in its honesty."

—*Publishers Weekly*

"[Coates] wields words with a rare grace that gives his story
an uncommon power ... A rare, lyrical family memoir."

—*Kirkus Review* (starred review)

"I grew up in a Maryland that lay years, miles, and worlds
away from the one whose summers and sorrows Ta-Nehisi
Coates evokes in this memoir with such tenderness and science; and the greatest proof of the power of this work is the
way that, reading it, I felt that time, distance, and barriers
of race and class meant nothing. That in telling his story he
was telling my own story, for me."

—Michael Chabon, author of *The Yiddish
Policemen's Union* and *The Amazing
Adventures of Kavalier & Clay*

"A superb debut by an extraordinary young talent. Coates
describes with poetic eloquence another country that is,

most painfully, ours; the father who raised him is a smoldering fire whose boundless love reaches across the room; his older brother Bill is a willow tree, bent low against the wind, and young Coates a child who, without bitterness or rancor, bore witness to the flight of his own innocence. Here is a major young writing talent who writes with a stunning poetic awareness and gorgeous immediacy."

—James McBride, bestselling author of
The Color of Water

"*The Beautiful Struggle* is a searing and soulful memoir of a black father and his sons that tells the truth about the virtues and costs of the black freedom struggle. Ta-Nehisi Coates is a sharp-eyed, quick-witted observer whose haunting eloquence and lively intelligence introduce to us one of the most brilliant writers of his generation. If ever a book proved that there is complexity and transcendent humanity in the story of black boys becoming men in a world they didn't make, but which they have memorably shaped, *The Beautiful Struggle* is it."

—Michael Eric Dyson, author of *Know What I Mean?* and *Between God and Gangsta Rap*

"*The Beautiful Struggle* is an intoxicating reminder of why we carry worn paperbacks in our coat pockets and fall asleep with memoirs on our chests. We want to believe in the promise that great literature can make us see ourselves anew. With his lyrical language, zoom lens detail, and seductive story telling Ta-Nehisi Coates proves himself to be a promise keeper."

—Michael Datcher, author of
Raising Fences: A Black Man's Love Story

"Ta-Nehisi Coates's *The Beautiful Struggle* is a compelling story told in a musical voice about the author's father, a proud black man and revolutionary, struggling to raise his family in the ashes of the revolution. A timely story of family, tough love, and courage."

—Flores Forbes, author of *Will You Die With Me?: My Life and the Black Panther Party*

"A beautiful journey. A voice rich in detail, Coates is lyrical and clever. As he navigates through a slice of urban America, we root for him as he fumbles and finds purpose. This debut establishes Coates as one of the most luminous storytellers of his generation."

—Natalie Y. Moore, author of *Deconstructing Tyrone: A New Look at Black Masculinity in the Hip-Hop Generation*

"A beautiful story of manhood from a beautiful American city, where emotions fall as hard as rain and can prove to be just as cleansing. But the most remarkable thing in *The Beautiful Struggle* is the voice of Ta-Nehisi Coates, which lingers in the ear. A find you're not likely to forget."

—Neely Tucker, author of *Love in the Driest Season*

"With humor, grace, and an impressive reserve of compassion, Ta-Nehisi Coates has crafted a great gift of a book. *The Beautiful Struggle* should be required reading for black boys—and those who are raising one."

—William Jelani Cobb, author of *The Devil and Dave Chappelle*

By Ta-Nehisi Coates

Between the World and Me
The Beautiful Struggle

the
beautiful
struggle

a memoir

ta-nehisi coates

Spiegel & Grau

New York

2009 Spiegel & Grau Trade Paperback Edition

Copyright © 2008 by Ta-Nehisi Coates

All rights reserved.

Published in the United States by Spiegel & Grau, an imprint of
Random House, a division of Penguin Random House LLC, New York.

SPIEGEL & GRAU and the HOUSE colophon are registered trademarks of
Penguin Random House LLC.

Originally published in hardcover in the United States by Spiegel & Grau,
an imprint of Random House, a division of Penguin Random House LLC,
in 2008.

Library of Congress Cataloging-in-Publication Data

Coates, Ta-Nehisi.
The beautiful struggle / Ta-Nehisi Coates.
p. cm.
ISBN 978-0-385-52746-0
eBook ISBN 978-0-385-52684-5
1. Coates, Ta-Nehisi. 2. African Americans—
Maryland—Baltimore—Biography. 3. African
Americans—Maryland—Baltimore—Social conditions.
4. Fathers and sons—Maryland—Baltimore—Biography.
5. Street life—Maryland—Baltimore.
6. Baltimore (Md.)—Biography. I. Title.

F189.B153C63 2008
975.2'6004960730092—dc22
[B]   2007052166

Printed in the United States of America on acid-free paper

randomhousebooks.com
spiegelandgrau.com

22 24 26 28 30 29 27 25 23

Book design by Donna Sinisgalli
Map design and illustration by Jackie Aher

This is for my mother,
Cheryl Waters

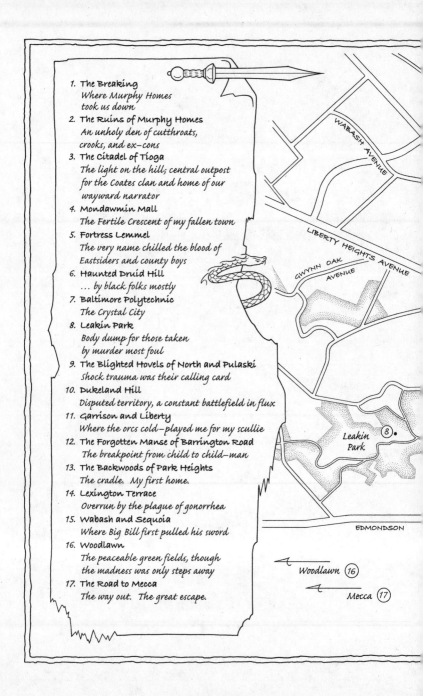

1. **The Breaking**
   Where Murphy Homes
   took us down
2. **The Ruins of Murphy Homes**
   An unholy den of cutthroats,
   crooks, and ex-cons
3. **The Citadel of Tioga**
   The light on the hill; central outpost
   for the Coates clan and home of our
   wayward narrator
4. **Mondawmin Mall**
   The Fertile Crescent of my fallen town
5. **Fortress Lemmel**
   The very name chilled the blood of
   Eastsiders and county boys
6. **Haunted Druid Hill**
   ... by black folks mostly
7. **Baltimore Polytechnic**
   The Crystal City
8. **Leakin Park**
   Body dump for those taken
   by murder most foul
9. **The Blighted Hovels of North and Pulaski**
   Shock trauma was their calling card
10. **Dukeland Hill**
    Disputed territory, a constant battlefield in flux
11. **Garrison and Liberty**
    Where the orcs cold-played me for my scullie
12. **The Forgotten Manse of Barrington Road**
    The breakpoint from child to child-man
13. **The Backwoods of Park Heights**
    The cradle. My first home.
14. **Lexington Terrace**
    Overrun by the plague of gonorrhea
15. **Wabash and Sequoia**
    Where Big Bill first pulled his sword
16. **Woodlawn**
    The peaceable green fields, though
    the madness was only steps away
17. **The Road to Mecca**
    The way out. The great escape.

WABASH AVENUE

LIBERTY HEIGHTS AVENUE

GWYNN OAK AVENUE

Leakin Park (8)

EDMONDSON

Woodlawn (16)

Mecca (17)

the coates clan

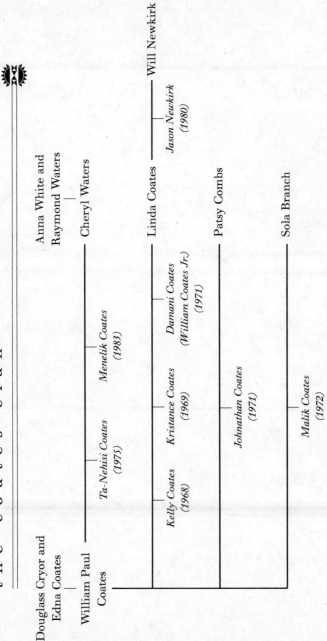

Douglass Cryor and
Edna Coates

William Paul
Coates

Anna White and
Raymond Waters

Cheryl Waters

Ta-Nehisi Coates
(1975)

Menelik Coates
(1983)

Kelly Coates
(1968)

Kristance Coates
(1969)

Damani Coates
(William Coates Jr.)
(1971)

Linda Coates

Will Newkirk

Jason Newkirk
(1980)

Johnathan Coates
(1971)

Patsy Combs

Malik Coates
(1972)

Sola Branch

CHAPTER 1

There lived a little boy who was misled . . .

When they caught us down on Charles Street, they were all that I'd heard. They did not wave banners, flash amulets or secret signs. Still, I could feel their awful name advancing out of the lore. They were remarkable. They sported the Stetsons of Hollis, but with no gold. They were shadow and rangy, like they could three-piece you—jab, uppercut, jab—from a block away. They had no eyes. They shrieked and jeered, urged themselves on, danced wildly, chanted

Rock and Roll is here to stay. When Murphy Homes closed in on us, the moon ducked behind its black cloak and Fell's Point dilettantes shuffled in boots.

It was their numbers that tipped me off—no one else rolled this deep. We were surrounded by six to eight, but up and down the street, packs of them took up different corners. I was spaced-out as usual, lost in the Caves of Chaos and the magic of Optimus Prime's vanishing trailer. It took time for me to get clear. Big Bill made them a block away, grew tense, but I did not understand, even after they touched my older brother with a right cross so awkward I thought it was a greeting.

I didn't catch on till his arms were pumping the wind. Bill was out. Murphy Homes turned to me.

In those days, Baltimore was factional, segmented into crews who took their names from their local civic associations. Walbrook Junction ran everything, until they met North and Pulaski, who, craven and honorless, would punk you right in front your girl.

Above them all, Murphy Homes waved the scepter. The scale of their banditry made them mythical. Wherever they walked—Old Town, Shake and Bake, the harbor— they busted knees and melted faces. Across the land, the name rang out: Murphy Homes beat niggers with gas nozzles. Murphy Homes split backs and poured in salt. Murphy

Homes moved with one eye, flew out on bat wings, performed dark rites atop Druid Hill.

I tried to follow Bill, but they cut me off. A goblin stepped out from the pack—

Fuck, you going, bitch?

—and stunned me with a straight right. About that time my Converse turned to cleats and I bolted, leaving dents and divots in the concrete. The streetlights flickered, waved as I broke ankles, blew by, and when the bandits reached to check me, I left only imagination and air. I doubled back to Lexington Market. There was no sign of Bill. I reached for a pay phone.

Dad, we got banked.

Okay, Son, find an adult. Stand next to an adult.

I'm in front of Lexington Market. I lost Bill.

Son, I'm on the way.

I had crossed a border. This was more than Dad's black leather belt—I knew how that would end. But word to Tucker's Kobolds, this thing filing out across the way, lost boys with a stake in only each other, stretching down the block in packs, berserking everywhere, was awful and random. I stood near a man about Dad's age waiting at a bus stop, like age could shield me. He looked over at me unfazed and then back across the streets at the growing fray of frenzied youth.

———

We'd come out that night in search of the wrestlers, who were our latest sensation. They elevated bar fights to a martial art, would rush the ring, all juiced on jeers and applause, white music blaring, Van Halen hair waving in the wind, and raise their chins until their egos were eye level with God. Moves were invented, named, patented, and feared—heaven help Bob Backlund in the camel clutch— and we loved that, too, the stew of language that gave a beat down style and grace, that made an eye gouge a ritual.

You could find us, noon on Saturdays, sprawled out on the living room floor, adjusting the hanger behind our secondhand color TV, until the Fabulous Freebirds, Baby Doll, and Ron Garvin emerged from the wavy lines and static. The wrestlers barnstormed the country perfecting their insane number. They were confused. They ranted with the rhythm of black preachers; wore silk robes, bikinis, and spangled belts; carried parasols; and recited poetry. Glossy mags sprung up from nothing, spread their gospel, their scowling mugs, their hollow threats and lore. They gave dressing room interviews, punctuated by jab at the air. Whole histories were pillaged, myths bastardized, until Hercules Hernandez stepped off Olympus and the Iron Sheik delivered the Mideast to the Midwest. They held summits and negotiations, all of these ending in a rain of blows.

Other fans had their Hulksters or the golden Von Erichs. But for me only the American Dream could endure.

He waddled down the aisle, bathed in applause and fireworks. His gut poured over bikini trunks. His eyes were black histories.

The Horsemen would tie the Dream to the ropes, beat him until his hair was a mop of bloody blond. I'd cringe and pound the floor, yelling for him to get up. But Bill always rooted for villains, and cackled as Ric Flair strutted the ring, flipping his wig of platinum blond. Then the Dream would dig in, reverse figure fours, throw bionic elbows and Sonny Liston rights. In the midst of his fleeing adversaries—the battered Tully Blanchards and shattered Andersons—he'd look out at the crowd gone mad and snatch the mic like KRS—

It's me, the Great. The king of the ring. Like I told you, the Dream *IS* professional wrestling. I have been to the mountaintop, and it will take a hell of a man to knock me off.

We had to see them. But that road went right through Dad, whose only point in life was toil. He worked seven days a week. Big Bill called him the pope, for weekly he issued sweeping edicts like he had a line to God. He outlawed eating on Thanksgiving, under pain of lecture. He disavowed air-conditioning, VCRs, and Atari. He made us cut the grass with a hand-powered mower. In the morning he'd play NPR and solicit our opinions just to contravene and debate. Once, over a series of days, he did the math on Tarzan and the Lone Ranger until, at six, I saw the dull taint of colonial power. I am sure this is what brought him comically to our side.

With two tickets to live pro wrestling, he offered a gift and a joke—

Go see Kamala the Ugandan Giant. And you will understand, as I do, that that nigger is from Alabama.

At the Baltimore Arena we were in full effect. We peered down from cheap seats so high that the ring was our own gift box. There were white people everywhere, and this was the most I'd ever seen of them. They wore caps and jeans sliced into shorts; herded kids, hot dogs, and popcorn. I thought they looked dirty, and this made me racist and proud.

I'd like to tell you what immediately happened next. But I don't remember. I was open, and wanted to cheer the Birdman, resplendent in wraparound shades, a Jheri curl, and fluorescent gold-and-blue spandex. He was always oblivious to his theme music. His tune was internal, and maybe that night he dipped and glided toward the ring, flapping his arms and talking to the parakeets perched on each of his shoulders. I wanted to see the Dream, who was at the height of his feud with the Horsemen, and outnumbered, had taken to guerrilla warfare—masks, capes, am-

6

bushes, beef extended into parking lots, driveways and dream dates. But I lost it all out there, and when I dig for that night, all that emerges are the tendrils of Murphy Homes, how they dug into my brother's head. He was already a kid of the streets. But this highway robbery, this thievery of your own person, pushed him toward something else. He was touched by the desperate, and now fully comprehended the stakes.

I know that Dad and Ma saved me, pulled up in their silver Rabbit, some time after I made the call; that Dad ran off into the swarming night to find his eldest son, and for the first and only time, I was afraid for him. I know that Bill's mother, Linda, swooped down to the harbor and found Bill first, shuttled him back out to their crib in Jamestown. I know that Bill returned to Tioga days later, and when I told him how I'd dusted Murphy Homes, how I was on some Kid Flash shit, he was incredulous—

Fool, they let you get away so they could chase me.

If the newspapers Dad left around the house were true, the greater world was obsessed over *Challenger* and the S&L scandal. But we were another country, fraying at our seams. All the old rules were crumbling around us. The statistics were dire and oft recited—1 in 21 killed by 1 in 21, more of us in jail than college.

A cottage industry sprung up to consider our fate. Jawanza Kunjufu was large in those days, his book *Countering the Conspiracy to Destroy Black Boys* promised answers and so was constantly invoked. At conferences, black boys were assembled. At schools we were herded into auditoriums. At home, mothers summoned us to dinner tables, and there they delivered the news: Our time was short.

We lived in a row house in the slope of Tioga Parkway in West Baltimore. There was a small kitchen, three bedrooms, and three bathrooms—but only one that anybody ever wanted to use. All of us slept upstairs. My folks in a modest master. My two sisters, Kris and Kell—when back from Howard University, in an area where Dad also stored his books. There was a terrace out back, with a rotting wooden balcony. I almost died out there one day. Leaning against the crumbling wood I tumbled headlong, but caught myself on the back door roof and came lucky feet-first to the ground.

My room was the smallest, and always checkered with scattered volumes of World Book, Childcraft, Dragonlance, and Narnia. I slept on bunk beds made from thick pine, shared the bottom with my baby brother Menelik. Big Bill, as in all things, was up top. By mere months, he was my father's first son, but he turned this minor advantage into heraldry. He began sentences with "As the oldest son . . ." and sought to turn all his younger siblings into warriors. Big Bill was seldom scared. He had a bop that moved the crowd, and preempted beef. When bored, he'd entertain himself, cracking on your busted fade, acne, or your off-brand kicks.

Bill: Ta-Nehisi, get the fuck outta here with those weak-ass N.B.A.s. Know what that shit stands for? Next time buy Adidas. And, Gary, I don't know what you laughing at in those four-stripe Cugas. Know what that means? Nigger, can u get Adidas . . .

In those days, crazy Chuckie threatened our neighborhood. When we lined up for five on five, every tackle he took personally, every block was an invite to scrap. Once he pulled a metal stake from the ground, swung it at fat Wayne until he retreated all the way into our living room. That's when Dad came out and revealed the face of This Is Not a Game. Chuckie cursed and waved the stake. Then he stalked off. That night I lay on the bottom bunk, replaying it all for Bill.

Me: Man, Chuckie is crazy.

Bill: Fuck Chuckie. If he ever step to me, I'll fuck him up.

That fall, Chuckie killed his father, got gaffled by the jakes, and disappeared into the netherworld of Boys' Village or Hickey Juvenile.

Private school Stevie lived two doors down. I'd sit outside playing with his G.I. Joes until I realized that this made me a target. Across the street was Mondawmin Mall, the fashion seat of West Baltimore, the pit of sex, beat downs, and cool. Every window glittered with leather, fur, sterling, and stickers with large red numbers and slash marks. But the price tags and fat-ass honeys made boys turn killer. One misstep onto suede Pumas, and the jihad begins. In those days cocaine was the air, and though I never saw a fiend fire up, the smoke darkened everything, turned our homey town into a bazaar of cheap ornaments bought expensively, a Gomorrah on the inner harbor. A young man's worth was the width of his blond cable-link chain. The space between two, three, then four finger rings marked footmen from cavalry, cavalry from the great gentry of this darker age. In all our dreams we cruised the avenue in black Cherokee Jeeps, then parked at the corner of Hot and Live, our system flogging eardrums, pumping "Latoya" and "Sucker MCs." Even I shared those dreams, and I was only ten.

While I was hobbled by preteen status and basic nature, Big Bill was enthralled by the lights. This was the summer of '86. KRS-One laid siege to Queensbridge. I would stand in my bedroom, throwing up my hands, reciting the words of Todd Smith—"Walkin' down the street, to the hardcore beat/While my JVC vibrates the concrete." Bill and my brother John spent all summer busing tables. Bill schemed on a fat rope, one that dangled from his neck like sin. Still, his money was young, and he could not stomach the months of layaway. So he returned from the mall with two mini-ziplock bags, each the size of a woman's fist, each glimmering, like him, in the light. They held massive rings, one adorned with a golden kite, another spanning two fingers, molded into a dollar sign.

He flashed them before me, and I was caught by how the glowing metal made him swell inside his own skin. He was profiling, lost in all his glory, when Dad stepped to him.

Dad: Son. They're fake. Son, you've been had.

Bill: You're bugging. This is fourteen-karat. I paid cash money.

Dad: Son, Son. Let's have them smelted down and tested. If it's ten karats or more, I will pay you for the rings. With interest.

Bill's head went reeling, the dream within reach: He saw a gold herringbone spread over his Black BVD, and when he bopped through Mondawmin, jennys would jump on his jock and soldiers would collapse or salute. In the order of Slick Rick, Bill would wear the scarlet robe. So he agreed to my father's proposition, convinced he was on the better end. We were young, drunk on ourselves, and could not know that all the alleys we took as original, he'd stepped through before. He found a place to smelt the gold, do the math. And I don't know what was worse—the negative results or Dad's rueful chuckle and sermon. Afterward, Dad went over to Mondawmin and had Bill point out the merchants. Then he walked to the glass counter, brandished the results, and spoke magic words. The magic words were "fraud," "Black community," and "State's attorney." Bill never felt the same about gold again.

My father was Conscious Man. He stood a solid six feet, was handsome, mostly serious, rarely angry. Weekdays, he scooted out at six and drove an hour to the Mecca, where he guarded the books and curated the history in the exalted hall of the Moorland-Spingarn Research Center. He was modest—brown slacks, pale yellow shirt, beige Clarks—and hair cut by his own hand.

But at night, he barbecued tofu, steamed basmati, and thought of sedition. He'd untuck his shirt and descend into the cellar, then comb through layers of ancient arcana. He collected out-of-print texts, obscure lectures, and self-published monographs by writers like J. A. Rogers, Dr. Ben, and Drusilla Dunjee Houston, great seers who returned Egypt to Africa and recorded our history, when all the world said we had none. These were words that *they* did not want us to see, the lost archives, secret collections, folders worn yellow by water and years. But Dad brought them back.

From the day we touched these stolen shores, he'd explain to anyone who'd listen, they infected our minds. They deployed their phrenologists, their backward Darwinists, and forged a false Knowledge to keep us down. But against this demonology, there were those who battled back. Universities scorned them. Compromised professors scoffed at their names. So they published themselves and hawked their Knowledge at street fairs, churches, and bazaars.

For their efforts, they were forgotten. Their great works languished out of print, while those they sought to save grew fat on integration and amnesia.

Dad tracked the autodidacts and relatives of the ones who'd passed. Over tea in their living rooms, he unfurled his ambition. Dad proposed restoring these lost geniuses to their esteemed chairs in the university without walls, through a publishing operation he built from saddle-stitch staplers, a table-top press, and a Commodore 64. Never had republishing been so radical. He called this basement operation Black Classic Press, and for the Coates family there was no escape. All of that house was bent by the mad dream of mass resurrection.

He covered the crib with Knowledge, until rooms overflowed with books whose titles promised militant action and the return to glory. *Wonderful Ethiopians* and *Black Egypt and Her Negro Pharaohs*. He found others like him, formed collectives, held festivals in honor of Malcolm X and Marcus Garvey and the taking of arms. Brothers and sisters would drum and dance the unearthed rhythms, poets revealed words with teeth. Even the food was conscious—wheat bread and veggie burgers, cookies sweetened by fruit. Dad just played the back, peering from behind his table covered with African cloth and the awesome spread of books brought back from the dead.

This bounty drew the survivors, the ones who outlasted Hoover and COINTELPRO. They approached the tables with expectations so great that they dispensed even with English, opting for Swahili, Arabic, or Twi. All week they swept streets, worked day care, drove buses, taught piano, counseled the high school youth. You would know them by their dreads, their stoicism, the scent of sandalwood and licorice.

They would see me hustling books at these affairs with Ma or Big Bill, and go to school, because the Movement was all that they were. They'd start with the significance of Nkrumah or assail us for not carrying books by Dr. Clarke. They'd pause for libations, shout for Bunchy Carter, Nat Turner, and Aunt Grace. Then mellowed by the ancestors, they would smile. I was Coates's boy, though they did not know which one. I was young, and unconcerned with why Denmark Vesey did not come off, how the Belgians tackled Lumumba, or the slave-king Sakura's return.

But out on the block, the hoppers draped themselves in Starter, Diadora, and Lottoes. Then they'd roll onto corners and promptly clutch their nuts. Big Bill was there. He rolled through the streets in a brown puff leather, and captained a minor gang of Mondawmin kids. When bored, they brought the ruckus, snatching bus tickets and issuing beat downs at random. They gave no reason. They published no manifestos. This was how they got down. This was the ritual.

They spent summers hunting for girls. The jennys

would catwalk through Mondawmin in stonewash with wide red hands spray-painted across their asses. They gilded their namesakes in triple bamboo earrings, and when they heard your call—hey, yo, shortie, come here—they did not look back to flip a bird. They did not crack smiles for anything. Their focus was on hair, mounds and mounds of hair, gelled, fried, french rolled, finger waved, extended into a dyed and glittered crown. They were of the moment. They took one look at West Baltimore and understood that they were the best of it. So they walked like they were all that mattered, like they had no time.

You had to be harder then. You could not bop through Park Heights like the second coming of Peanut King. Even the skating rinks demanded six deep. Lexington Terrace was hot with gonorrhea. Teen pregnancy was the fashion. Husbands were outties. Fathers were ghosts.

Here's the cast of my last name: My father has seven kids by four women. Some of us were born to best friends. Some of us were born in the same year. My elders come first, in chronology: Kelly, Kris, William Jr.—all born of my father's first marriage to Linda.

John was born to Patsy, Malik born to Sola.

Then me and Menelik, the children of my mother, Cheryl. This is all a mess on paper, but it was all love to me, and formed my earliest and still enduring definition of family.

Big Bill and John were both born in 1971. Dad was married and two daughters deep. He was a veteran, and must have seemed to Linda to be a stand-up ordinary guy. But he lurched radical and enlisted in that subgeneration overwhelmed by the rigid ethics of picketing elders and the creaking pace of change. He joined the Black Panther Party, rose to lead the local chapter. He lost his union job. He went to work overtime for the impending revolution. His family went on relief.

Dad missed the birth of Kris and Kell, and was away again when Linda went into labor with Big Bill. Something always seemed to happen—a phone was off the hook, one of the Panthers took a shoddy message. On the day of Bill's birth, Dad pushed Linda's 1966 Mustang across town to South Baltimore General. He was carrying some measure of spiritual weight. He was twenty-five, at the height of all his vigor, and out to get his share. He lived with Linda and the kids at the top of a winding road out in South Baltimore's Cherry Hill. But he wore no rings, felt marriage was day-to-day, and was out to fulfill the general destiny of young men, and the particular one of his father.

The Panthers brought politics to match his studly quest. They lived in a commune, shared socks, and swapped beds. They were comrades, partners in the great unmaking, the fall of families, governments, economies defined by systems of profit and greed. In this new world, nothing was stamped as exclusive. Dad took to this naturally, and soon it seemed whenever a woman smiled his way, she'd already begun dividing her life into trimesters.

What Linda knew of the Panthers was that Dad had gone from honorable, hardworking vet to someone who justified food stamps and the projects. Dad arrived at the hospital the night Bill was born, and found his wife laid up and lovely in all her postpartum glow, and that made him confessional and bold. He had planned no speech, or special way, but just blurted it like bad soup: Linda, I have another child on the way. There was no good time to drop this, but there were many really bad ones and Dad had picked from this lot.

Even young, Dad had more vision than most for the big picture, but paired this with a stunning blindness for the intricacies of actual people. So he performed this ignominious feat again. That October, he came to the hospital to see Patsy and newborn John. Again he found a mother of his child laid up. Again he dropped the same load but with a twist. He had another child on the way, by Patsy's best friend and comrade in the party.

My father knew how to hurt people without knowing how he'd hurt them. And maybe in the end this is what saved him. He was shameless in his pursuit of women. He was perpetually broke. But he never shirked when his bill came due. He hustled for his baby's new shoes, while his frayed at the seams. Among the Conscious, he was known for the books he exhumed and breathed back. But he was known just as much for the constant presence of his brood, even as the specific makeup of the brood rotated. This is a low bar, I know. But we lived in an era of chronic welchers, where the disgrace was so broad that niggers actually bragged of running out on kids.

You could find my father at the kitchen table shaking his head at the Sunday paper, in the living room stewing over the evening news. His charges were five boys and two girls, and when he died, they would be his only words. He was called to fatherhood like a tainted preacher. The root was his own alcoholic father, who seeded so many children that Dad simply lost count. He impregnated three sisters, and so Dad had aunts doubling as stepmothers.

His father was intellectual, forced him to recite Bible verses, lectured from the morning paper. But anger and cheap wine soiled the best of him. He'd snap on a dime and fling five-year-old Dad clear across the living room. Aunt Pearl would step up and take the beating for him. When he was nine, Dad came home from school and found his life out on the sidewalk. He spent the following weeks living in a pickup truck with his father, two brothers, and Aunt Pearl. Later his father dropped him and his brother David off at his mother's house and faded out.

Now Dad had woven his own tangle of mothers and children spanning fourteen years. His passion was sons, if only because the odds and stakes seemed so high. We held him in this weird place, somewhere between hatred and complete reverence. All our friends were fatherless, and Dad was some sort of a blessing, but he made it hard to feel that way. He was a practicing fascist, mandating books and banning religion. Once he caught Big Bill praying at the kitchen table and ordered him to stop—

You want to pray, pray to me. I put the food on this table.

Another time, in the middle of dinner, Bill pronounced that he couldn't wait to grow up so he could move out, make his own rules. Dad stared hard—

You don't have to wait. You can go now.

All of us knew he was flawed, but still he retained the aura of a prophet. On our life map, he drew a bright circle around twelve through eighteen. This was the abyss where, unguided, black boys were swallowed whole, only to re-emerge on corners and prison tiers.

Dad was at war with this destiny. He was raising soldiers for all terrain. He preached awareness, discipline, and confidence. He went upside heads for shirking chores, for reaching across the table for the hush puppies, for knocking over a pitcher of juice. His technique was random—you might get away with a sermon on the virtues of Booker T., or a woman he left behind in Vietnam. Or you might catch the swinging black leather belt.

Once, Bill and me got to wrestling on Ma and Dad's bed, and some of the boards in the frame snapped in two. We engineered a sloppy resetting. Dad and Ma wouldn't be home till after we'd gone to bed. If Dad asks, Bill instructed, just tell him you don't know what happened.

Dad woke me up first. What happened to the bed?

I shrugged. I don't know . . .

He woke up Bill. What happened to the bed?

We broke it wrestling.

I glared, but only inside.

You had to make it worse by lying, Dad said.

He took us downstairs to the back door. Both of you get out. Go out back. You want to wrestle, go out in the backyard right now and wrestle.

Then he shut the door. We stared at each other for a moment, then Bill grabbed me and threw me to the ground. We tangled out there on the dirt for Dad's benefit for who knows how long, before we realized that he probably wasn't watching.

Ma came out later, sent us back upstairs. Dad had gone to bed.

My father scared me, but not even fear could alter the basics of nature. I brought home mediocre report cards: *Is not working up to potential, Needs to apply himself, Discipline is a problem.* Ma would go up to school and come back with migraines—that she passed on to us. Her eyes would go white. She'd dig nails into my arm—

I am not raising nothing niggers. Where is your head? What are you thinking, boy?

I am thinking of Sunday waffles and Morning Star. I am grieving for Lynn Min-mei, apatosaurs, Tom Landry, and Cowboy blue. I am staring three desks over and dreaming of Brenda Neil, dancing in a pink and white gown.

Dad would see me coming like some great lost cause, and clap his hands thrice—

Wake up, boy. Walk like you got business. Walk like you got somewhere to be.

I had my chances to turn this story another way. In fourth grade, Ma and Dad sent me off to apply for scholarships at private schools. I went through the rounds of class visits, noted how much better the lunch was, and then dawdled my way through the standardized tests. I was bigger than multiple choice and bubbles, so I picked answers at

22

random and acted shocked when months later I was rejected by every school.

Now two years later Dad's methods grew radical. William H. Lemmel Middle School sat on a hill off Dukeland. From its depths, wild rumors spewed—vice principals body-slammed on open fields, atrocities perpetrated in lunch lines, boys walking home in socks. But at Lemmel, the teachers waged Dad's kind of fight. Across the state, better jobs, better salaries, better living called out to them. But in the midst of Reconstruction's second collapse, Lemmel fought back. The headmasters arranged their students into teams, and named each one after the Saints—Douglass, Tubman, Woodson, King. They mandated uniforms, formed classes for the ghetto's gifted, and trumpeted their ostentatious mantra—Lemmel Middle School Is a School for Winners. This redoubled Dad's efforts, reinforced his mission to ground me in history and struggle. But when Big Bill heard this, he gave me the only words that mattered: Lemmel niggers don't play.

Big Bill was now a permanent fixture at Tioga, having been remanded from the good graces of his mother. His time was running out. He was entering tenth grade. He was tall and smooth as Kane touching "All Night Long." He pulled shorties with all the effort of a long yawn, and, like so many, believed that he would make a living off his jumper.

It must have been that summer of fool's gold, when Bill and John went extreme. They worked together busing tables at a local deli. One Saturday they left work and went riding in a stolen car with our cousin Gary. That evening Dad was informed that his sons were in the custody of the Baltimore county police. Dad drove out to get his boys, and when he had them back at home, he administered a legendary thrashing. The next morning, Dad unfurled a list of labors, and Tioga turned into a work camp. More so even than usual. About that time Bill was permanently assigned a bedroom, which he shared with me and Menelik, who was four. He laced the walls with autographed posters of his favorite ballers, the Human Highlight Reel and the Big Smooth.

Now Ma checked my and Bill's homework every night. Dad ran a compulsory book-of-the-month club selected from what we considered obscure and irrelevant. Bill requested back issues of *Sports Illustrated*. I don't even remember Dad replying. But I do remember *Flight to Canada* and Dad's attempts to inculcate us with Ishmael Reed's unique brand of humor. Bill had his own jokes—

Look at that guffed-up trim, he said, pointing to Reed's back-cover portrait. This nigger's got a half fro.

On weekend evenings, released from Dad's yoke, we would sit out on the front porch with the radio pumping

New York straight talk. Frank Ski would take to the one and twos, and drive off Whitney and all the feminized rhythm and bullshit, until Afrika Bambaataa owned the night. Bill would pop a tape into the second deck of his boom box. He'd tagged his moniker—M.C. Destiny—to both speakers with white out. Some nights Dante, from two doors down, would step past his staggering father and come hang. Once, when lifted, Dante's Dad tried to fit his key into our front door. Dad opened and politely directed him home, then silenced Bill, who'd gone up the steps cackling.

Dante would give Bill some dap—I was not yet worthy—and sit down on the brick steps, nodding to "The Show" or "Paul Revere." He had it bad for our older sister Kris, and he would groan and razz Bill about this fact. But Bill was too cool. He'd just laugh and search Dante for imperfections—ears like Hawaiian Islands, a scuffed pair of Adidas—and crack on him for an hour. Then he'd punch Dante in the arm, Get off my porch, punk. They were like all the neighborhood laughing boys. Around the corner, the gaping maw of the world waited and they had no idea.

Dad would be in the basement working with his books. He could not understand that we too were unearthing, that we were beholders of sorcery—Phil Collins mixed with the Biz, Ofra Haza, and The God.

———

Dad left the Panthers in '72 and was awarded the lofty title "Enemy of the People." This was shortly after he first met my mother. He would pack his car with Knowledge of Self and drive over to Howard University. He set up a table, and on it displayed many volumes of concealed history and radical lore. In those days, Howard was the fountain of all things right with the Race. The school had grown strong under Jim Crow, feasted on the minds of students and teachers color-bound to a handful of schools, until it was more than a University but a Mecca, and was known as such by all who were down. In the '50s and '60s Brothers came to the Mecca, thinking only of their nether selves, for it was said that at no point in history had there been more beautiful women in one place than at any random day on that campus. But somehow they were changed there, and left possessed by the spirit of Howard's legendary professoriat, of Eric Williams and E. Franklin Frazier, and they fled South to be flogged by sheriffs and Klansmen.

Now in the days after Malcolm and Martin, the Mecca was changing again. Dad sold books at conferences that promised a new order, ushered in by poetry, independent schools, and bricks. But more than all the new slang and ways of being he beheld, it was an elder who gave the lesson that pointed out the path for his kids. This man had worked at Howard in a low honorable way, sweeping the floors, raking the grass, sanctifying the toilets. I know nothing of his life, except that he found great peace that the Mecca's bylaws granted a free education to all children of the school's employees. Dad heard this and was struck. Now many years later, he'd procured a job working in Moorland-Spingarn. With seven kids the need was extreme. But already my sisters Kris and Kelly were enrolled. What was left were five boys, two of us sitting out there nodding to this new and lovely noise.

It was the sound of our era, and in it we beheld all our wants and great fears. Big Bill was under pressure. Murphy Homes had left him exposed and open to the knowledge that there were many moments when all he would have was himself. This was 1986 onset of the Crack Age. People started dying all around us—Nana, Aunt Joyce, Bill's grandmother Ms. Verla, and then the record 250 other Baltimoreans gone missing by murder. That year, my man Craig was butchered on his way home from work. He was the poorest kid in a class where everyone was on lunch tickets. His shoes talked; he wore a red plaid lumberjack shirt many days out of the week. He had several siblings. Now the orcs had ambushed and taken him out.

I came into all of this dazed by the lack of shade, by the quickness between child and child-man. But, as always,

Big Bill was clear, and after Murphy Homes he probed his connections until he found a merchant of arms. He stashed it in our bedroom, in his brown puff leather jacket. He showed it to me without bravado, its weight gave it authority, and I knew it was real. And from that point forward when walking the land, my brother Big Bill was strapped.

=====

CHAPTER 2

Even if it's jazz or the quiet storm . . .

When crack hit Baltimore, civilization fell. Dad told me how it used to be. In his time, the beefs were petty and stemmed from casual crimes: bopping too hard down an alien street, spitting game at somebody's little sister. There were gangs who lived to throw down, and, true, every full moon or so a killer would reach into his houndstooth coat and make it rain. But there were rules and even when Dad was caught off guard and faced with a hostile crew, he knew he could throw up his dukes and yell "fair one," and tackle their champion one-on-one. The bad end of a beef was loose teeth and stitches, rarely shock trauma and "Blessed Assurance" ringing the roof of the storefront funeral home.

In Dad's days, we were a close-knit circle, but a circle surrounded by dire wolves. All we had to hold us up was the next man. But as time went on, we forgot ourselves and went cannibal—the next brother became a meal to feed our rep. At night, *Action News* unfurled the daily scroll, and always amid the rescued dogs, the lost toddlers, the scandalous bankers, there was us, buckled by the pop-pop of a .22, laid out on a sad stain of blood.

I didn't fully get it then, but this was an inglorious turn. The world was filled with great causes—Mandela, Nicaragua, and the battle against Reagan. But we died for sneakers stitched by serfs, coats that gave props to teams we didn't own, hats embroidered with the names of Confederate states. I could feel the falling, all around. The flood of guns wrecked the natural order. Kids whose minds should have been on Teddy Ruxpin now held in their hands the power to dissolve your world into white. But Dad pledged to sire us through. With the aid of many mothers we were pushed through science camp, music lessons. Thick books were hurled at us from across the room.

In his tenth grade year, the year after ◌ Homes incident, Dad enrolled Big Bill in Upward ◌ one of the remnants of the Great Society and the da◌ when bureaucrats dreamed of free gas, water, and Ph.D.s for all who wanted. Bill was caged by a backward psychology. He saw himself strictly in the mode of athletes and rappers, and put no value on his own intellect and bookish wits. My father struggled to make Bill see what he covered with a street pose, what he didn't even know was there.

Saturday mornings, Upward Bound pulled Bill and a bevy of West Side kids up to the local community college to reinforce Pythagoras, Fitzgerald, and Newton. There was a freedom here—Upward Bound kids were sent by their parents, not ordered by the state, and so a certain level of bullshit was immediately cut out. Then in the summer, after weeks of taking college classes, they were treated to the full-blown campus experience out at Towson, where they stayed in dorms for the week.

This was Bill's first taste of university, the first time that it occurred to him that higher ed may not be beyond him. But this new idea didn't exactly exert a radical influence on him. My brother was immovable back then. He could be dead wrong and still steady talking to you like you'd never laced up Jordans or dribbled left. Once we spent the day at his mother's crib out in Jamestown, trying to destroy each other on Atari boxing. Presumably, I was left in his care, and though he knew the laws of Tioga banned the consumption of beef, he managed to convince me that a can of spaghetti and meatballs would pass Dad's muster.

Bill: Man, it's no big deal. When Dad comes he won't even know. And if he finds out, I'll just tell him. It's only once. What will he care?

Me: Okay.

But my brother's wits trailed his will, and when Dad came, he saw the emptied can, the two dirty bowls still in the sink. Of course, he went off, did not start swinging but let us know that we had violated. I sat on Linda's couch, absorbing the verbal onslaught, cursing how wrong my know-everything brother Bill was. Bill sat next to me, impassive, another lesson failing to connect.

He listened selectively, and cared most about his own internal compass, which he believed was attuned to the way the world should work. He was a bull, thought in straight lines, and though I found this trying, and I wasn't alone, his certitude engendered great respect. My brother was not reflective, but that made him unafraid. He would see you in a brawl, leap in swinging, but take many days to ask you what the fight was all about. Bill was a constant and

this won him allies wherever he dropped his B-more Bad-
boys cap.

In the dorms of Towson over that summer, he expanded his affiliations. He started hanging out further
north up Liberty Heights, at the corner of Wabash and Sequoia, about a mile from Mondawmin. He did not abandon
Tioga, but an aspiring king needed vassals from all over.
Your army was all you had, and the speed with which they
appeared when it went down, boosted or pruned your rep.
Bill's new friends—Marlon, Joey, Rock—were boys of our
ilk, stuck in that undefined place between the projects and
the burbs. They did not live in squalor. Their mothers tried
their best. But still they had to confront the winds of the
day. The most ordinary thing—the walk to school, a bike
ride around the block, a trip to the supermarket—could
just go wrong. And when it happened, we were only hands,
and those hands pledged to us, and then the fire some of us
kept between the belt buckle and waist.

When Bill was burned by Murphy Homes, he promised to never again be helpless. A rep was preventive medi-
cine. If you were from one of the lucky slums that struck
fear, you could walk where you pleased. It was what we all
wanted, even tender me, to be seen out there, and, on the
strength of my pedigree, turn any street into home field.

This was the motive for even Wabash, with its modest
lawns, brick homes, and absent public housing, to expect or

incite beef. Conflicts bloomed from a minor remark or misstep, and once in motion everyone stayed cocked and on alert. This is what beef is: Baltimore was too primitive for gangs, everything relied on natural or man-made borders. The duchy of Wabash and Sequoia was marked off by train tracks. North of there was Tawanda, a parallel world, that saw Wabash like Wabash saw them. You only crossed those tracks if you were out of your mind. Whatever you needed—cheesesteak, dish detergent, girls—you had on your requisite side.

It was night, and like all the others, Big Bill, Joey, and Marlon were out on their home corner. There was the normal high that comes from the hormones of youth, that fresh sense of being unchained. But also there was the omnipresent feeling that It could go down. In those moments—which back then were all of our moments—your neurology was always code red. Bill's crew was hypertensed—the laughter was controlled, smiles had edges, and no one stared too long at one spot.

And then It happened. Someone—no one ever remembers who—yelled, Yo, it's them, coming across the tracks.

There was no math. Bill just reached in his dip, and, like his friends, shot out in the appropriate direction.

He could have been a headline, some fool whose stray ripped through a bassinet. The rush blinded them, not one of them got eyes on a clear target. But in the yellow glare of streetlights, phantoms fell before them. Someone screamed "five-oh!" and there was a hectic dash down the now-quiet streets, up to Marlon's porch, and then down into his basement. They took a few breaths, settled some, and then got to yelling, high-fiving, and beating their chests. Yo, I hit one. Hell, yeah, I got at least two of 'em. When I heard about it, it sounded like something out of Looney Toons or the farcical West—a lot of gunfire, no blood or injuries. But that was not the point.

Bill heard the admonishments of my father, but Dad couldn't walk the path for him. We were divided—one foot in America, the other in a land of swords. They told us to act civilized, but everywhere bordered on carnage. Bill became uncomposed. To be strapped was to grab the steering wheel of our careening lives. A gun was a time machine and an anchor—it dictated events. To be strapped was to master yourself, to become more than a man whose life and death could be simply seized and hurled about.

Bill's logic was taken from the Great Knowledge, the sum experience of our ways from the time Plymouth Rock landed on us. To this compendium each generation added its volume. Our addition was the testament of the broken cities—West Side, Harlem, the fifth ward. The Knowledge

Man knew that death was jammed in us all, hell-bent on finding a way out. So he never measured his life in years but style—how he walked, who he walked with, how he stepped to jenny, where he was seen, where he was not. This man turned his life into art and pledged himself to the essential truth: No matter what Civilization says, academic intelligence is overpraised and ultimately we are animals. When I saw one of these true disciples, almost-men like my brother Bill, I knew there were vital things that I had missed.

The Knowledge was taught from our lives' beginnings, whether we realized it or not. Street professors presided over invisible corner podiums, and the Knowledge was dispensed. Their faces were smoke and obscured by the tilt of their Kangols. They lectured from sacred texts like Basic Game, Applied Cool, Barbershop 101. Their leather-gloved hands thumbed through chapters, like "The Subtle and Misunderstood Art of Dap." There was the geometry of cocking a baseball cap, working theories on what jokes to laugh at and exactly how loud; and entire volumes devoted to the crossover dribble. Bill inhaled the Knowledge and departed in a sheepskin cap and gown. I cut class, slept through lectures, and emerged awkward and wrong.

My first day at Lemmel, I was a monument to unknowledge. I walked to school alone, a severe violation of the natural order of things. I got my first clue of this standing on my front porch, my canvas backpack slid across one shoulder, watching as small groups of kids make their way down the green hill that sat at the end of the Mondawmin parking lot. All the way to school, everyone rolled like this—three deep or deeper. There was a warped affection among them, the kind born from a common threat. They constantly looked around. They tossed ice grills like there was no other choice. They exchanged pounds with each other frequently, as if to say I am here, I am with you. All their Starter caps were cocked at the appropriate angle. Everyone moved as though the same song were playing in their heads. It was a song I'd never heard. I shrugged my backpack a little tighter on my shoulder and made my way.

Later I'd understand that the subaudible beat was the Knowledge, that it kept you ready, prepared for anyone to start swinging, to start shooting. Back then, I had no context, no great wall against the fear. I felt it but couldn't say it.

I paid little heed to great injustice, despite my mother showing me blueprints of slave ships and children's books tracking the revolution of Dessalines and Toussaint. Still, I could spot even small injustices when they shadowed me personally. I knew that to be afraid while on the way to school was deeply wrong.

I walked the hill alone, the error of my way now dawning on me, but reached the doors of Lemmel with everything intact. I climbed the long flight of concrete steps and stood in a corner of the school, waiting on the bell, staring at the ground, trying to vanish.

I emerged into a morass of numbers and bureaucracy. Lemmel was partitioned into three grades, four tracks, and sixteen classes, ranging from special ed to gifted. Each track was then given the name of a champion—Harriet Tubman, Booker T. Washington, Carter G. Woodson. My class was 7-16. We were one of six gifted classes on the Thurgood Marshall Team. I don't know how gifted any of us were—more likely we had parents in the race, mothers who worked for the city, got their degrees from Coppin State. They'd gone far enough to know what was out there and what they'd missed in the manner of their coming up. These are the parents the intellectuals erase in their treatises on black pathology. But I saw them in effect at Lemmel, that and teachers always with an eye for children who were two seconds faster and seemed to be bound for something more than the corner or Jessup. From the hallway's rafters these teachers hung propaganda: *It is by choice not chance . . . that we choose to advance, The Marshall Team; We can achieve . . . We will achieve.*

The many problems of the city came to rest at the Lemmel's doorsteps. Kids hailed from the projects, foster care, from homes without lighting, from parents who still shut down Odells while their children ran the streets. Lemmel stood out, because all the chaos of West Baltimore swirled around it but never inside. The school's guardians believed in the vocabulary of motivation and self-help. Their favorite phrases featured words like "confidence," "push," and "achieve." They saw Lemmel as a barracks, themselves as missionaries called to convert us to the civilized way.

My homeroom was ruled by the crusader, Ms. Nichols, who traded her government name of Eleanor for the freed handle of Sadiquah. Dreads flowed down her back. Her skin was dark and smooth. She was like the women Dad and the rest of us sold books to, the ones who'd pore through the selection on the tables, convinced that something between their covers could close the gap. I could not have been in her class more than twenty minutes before she started to curse. It flowed from her natural—Oh, that's bullshit; fuck that. I giggled like the rest of the class, but not too hard because she bore the seal of black matrons. Her eyes held razors; she sliced into boys who talked out of turn. You could see she came from somewhere hard like Walbrook Junction, that she'd risen off the block, even if the block had not risen off of her. But she was a philosopher. She used the great breadth of social studies to hold forth on sex, vegetarians, Reagan, apartheid, Akhenaton, and the origins of God.

This was all my father wanted—for the long struggle

to wake us up to be present in class as it was at home. The struggle infused all his dealings with me. Whenever he could, he violated my weekends with his latest pet lesson.

Dad: Ta-Nehisi, cut off the cartoons. You're coming with me.

Me: Can I have another hour?

Dad: (*The Look of Not Playing.*)

Me: (*Cutting off the TV*) Okay. I'm getting my jacket.

And then we were off in the brown minivan, across the city, public radio our soundtrack, my father telling me again the story of black folks' slide to ruin. He would drive down North Avenue and survey the carryouts, the wig shops, the liquor stores and note that not a one was owned by anybody black. We would stop at Brother Kinya's printing shop, and Dad would sit down and talk that brother/nation/black talk.

When we got home, I'd go upstairs and flop on the bed. But Dad never knew when to quit. Instead, he'd call me down to the basement and assign another book, another history that traced our days from the Nile Valley to the Zulus' last stand. When I turned the pages, I could feel the Something More, like a smoldering fire across the room.

Days later Dad would ask for a report. But try as I might, I could only half remember what I'd read, and what I remembered I could not really recite. My dad's response—a sudden shining in his eyes at the sound of certain words or at my stuttering approximation of some crucial idea—suggested to me that even the little I retained had gold in it. But none of it made sense. I was young and could not see the weaponry my ancestors had left for me, the shield in the tall brown grass, the ax lying right next to the tree.

My math teacher was Ms. Chance, who seemed to love only her kids more than math. She had style: an almost Southern accent, red highlights, and acrid perfume. Her zeal was so complete that it pulled us in, made us brag to friends that here we were at twelve, and we knew what it meant to add with *letters*. She whizzed through lectures, held coach classes after school. She was not Conscious in the way of my father, but in a different way that I couldn't name but could spot from one hundred feet away: the general manner of black people who simply wanted to compete and see the good works of their own brought forth. I was my own greatest foe, she told me. She'd be off on quadratic equations, then catch me in her periphery with my head in the sky.

Ta-Nehisi, wake up.

I was not a studious boy. I came to conclusions easier than most, but was increasingly disappointed in the world as it was, so invested almost nothing in studying it. But what I was inspired to know, I learned. I read my social studies text like a great novel. I was a novice at algebra, but I was so drawn in by the promise of Ms. Chance that I showed for coach class until I brought home an 80 average, which counted for a triumph on my report card.

These were the exceptions. In second grade my teacher told my mother she suspected that I was mildly retarded. But at Lemmel I truly indulged. I slept through French class, dreaming of pencil fights and paper football. We were blessed with Latin, but I spent most my time talking out of turn and finding excuses to leave my seat. I probed teachers for weakness, then proceeded to make them believe that my parents were on drugs.

Walking home from Lemmel, I couldn't shake free of my native dreamy state. I thought of everything and noticed almost nothing around me. I could have stumbled just out of the reach of an onrushing fender and felt only a light breeze. Still, I was smart enough to start walking home with friends—Leroy and some others from around my way, about my age. We took the grass hill, but by the time we got to the bottom, I was usually lagging behind the pack. And that's where I discovered all that I'd been warned about, cracking knuckles and looking my way.

I saw only one of them at first, but these things were three-card monte, and you never knew if there were ten others in camouflage waiting for you to swing or stumble on a rock. He came to me like he had no ill will, but his talk of peace was a lie. While I slowly focused, he quickly explained his pretext for approaching me. He acted confused, looked at me like I had an answer. It could have been a cousin with a snatched chain, a younger brother banked down at the harbor. It didn't matter because it was fiction. It's true our laws had mostly forsaken us, but we were not without shame. In deference to the statutes of yore, a boy always had to state the offense before he and his friends started swinging. But in deference to the perverted times, the charges were always pulled from the air, excuses.

I didn't respond. I didn't know what was going on. Three more appeared, flustered, abandoning this fake diplomacy, and one of them, with yellow skin, in a maroon tee and jeans, stepped to me waving his hands—

Mutherfucker, what's up?

But by then my group saw I was missing, and made their way back. I was saved by Leroy, who happened to be in one of their classes—

Naw, yo, he cool.

They looked me up and down, and backed away.

Warm Fridays, like that one, always meant fight season. The climate pulled the boys out in their shell tops and sweat suits. Later I came to know the crew that rolled on me—the Mighty Hilton-Beys. Lemmel kids, but the type who slept through middle school and were usually done by tenth grade. What they lived for was after school, slouching sinister in front the 7-Eleven at the bottom of Dukeland hill. That was where the hoppers lifted Hostess and reached for the burgeoning asses of young girls.

There were any number of crews like them, carving up Lemmel into fiefdoms. They were assembled by shared neighborhoods, classes, and elementary schools. Their minds were made small by scrambling at the bottom. So they stood on bus stops, in subway stations, flocked to sidewalk sales, tipped drunks for fifths, and flocked to the Civic Center and bumrushed the show. They would lamp outside Mondawmin Mall, between the Crab Shack and Murray's Steaks, attempting to invent a rep.

I was raised on the struggle of elders—iron collars, severed feet, the rifle of dirty Harriet, and down through the years, the Muslims and regal Malcolm. But mostly what I saw around me was rank dishonor: cable and Atari plugged into every room, juvenile parenting, niggers sporting kicks with price tags that looked like mortgage bills. The Conscious among us knew the whole race was going down, that we'd freed ourselves from slavery and Jim Crow but not the great shackling of minds. The hoppers had no picture of the larger world. We thought all our battles were homegrown and personal, but, like an evil breeze at our back, we felt invisible hands at work, like someone else was still tugging at levers and pulling strings.

The vagueness of the struggle made most of these kids barbarians, but there were a few like myself who were still noncombatants. My cheeks were fat. I talked a lot, laughed in such a way that I gave the hardest kids around me permission to laugh. That same easiness made me soft, and as I bounced awkwardly through the crowd of ungifted kids on my way to class in the morning, I became a confirmation of all the most dangerous rumors about the Marshall Team. Most of the Marshall Team were from further south, where the new nastiness of the city had already settled into a natural and unquestioned state. They understood their place in this new ecology. But still they would not play dumb. They were sharper than their friends, uncles, and cousins. And a couple of them even combined that with the grace of the street. Charles Davis could glide into algebra with perfect rhythm and a black leather bomber on his back, one of the rare kids who knew how to carry a textbook like it was fashion.

But most of these kids learned early that they were not funny or fast. They might have a jump shot or a spin move when running back a kick. But their talents were mostly elsewhere, and the other boys and girls gave them no respect. But somewhere about third grade they got the message: Fists could equalize it all. That if they could raise their dukes, they could cut a lot of the bullshit. It did not matter if their jab was wild or the headlock was no more than a firm hug. That they stood instead of ran made them hard targets and served notice to the bandits that there was no free lunch. Now they'd survived the early battles of elementary school and were here at Lemmel, in the midst of a bad combination. There was the bubbling pubescent machismo that under most circumstances eventually resulted in blows. There was the absence of men and fathers, men who could teach nuance and intelligence to boys. There were the girls, now sprouting attitude and curves, who we all desperately wanted to impress. And then there was class 7-16—the Marshall Team—the school nerds, easy marks.

By then almost every boy in my class had heard the talk in the halls—that 7-16 was soft, that its boys could not hold their hallway down. So my classmates rolled a little thicker than usually required, since sooner or later, one of them was bound to be touched.

This is how the Marshall Team, Lemmel's best and brightest, became a gang. They assembled in their own area before school. They had their own table at lunch. They would throttle one another at random moments, testing for a weak link. In bathrooms and at lunch tables they'd beat on each other and critique the response, because all this was a dry run for what we faced outside.

But I was peace pipes and treaties. My style was to talk and duck. It was an animal tactic, playing dead in hopes that the predators would move on to an actual fight. It was the mark of unKnowledge, a basic misreading of nature and humanity. The fallacy was brought to light outside Ms. Hines's Latin class just before lunch. The 7-16 boys circled around us. Kwesi Smith stood a few feet away. We were both new to Lemmel, and we'd already bonded over this fact. But he was a quicker study and when 7-16 formed an arena around us, and my eyes frantically scanned the wall of boys for a doorway out, Kwesi put up his dukes because he understood.

I got to know Kwesi as time went on. He invited me to his home for cookouts and birthday dinners at fish spots near the bay. He was like me, wore Bugle Boys, parachute pants, turtleneck sweaters with brass medallions and cryptic branding like "Fifth Patrol."

All that was months later. Today was different. Someone—maybe Merrill, Gerald, or Leon—set this all in motion. They wanted a fight. A voice came through the crowd, said something like, Let's see if you can take this mutherfucker. I raised my fist, thought, *I'll only swing if he*—and that was it. I was in midthought when Kwesi reached in and slapped me across the jaw. The rest of the Marshall Team was changing classes. I heard the entire hallway laugh at once, then it echoed throughout the school, then the city, and somewhere else I felt Big Bill shaking his head.

It was disrespect—I didn't even warrant knuckles. I got in a few lazy tags before a teacher broke it up. But that's how it started—with a blow that didn't even hurt. At lunch the story reverberated across tables and into the line. People I did not know were retelling the episode in grander terms—

That nigger was like, What the fuck you goin' do, bitch. And Tana—this is how they shortened my name—busted out crying.

I felt my tenuous status slipping into dangerous territory. I tried to talk it down, but did not understand what had really happened. I would have had to murder Kwesi in the lunchroom to get back any respect.

From then on, I was the weakest of the marks, and my weakness was despised. By the gifted kids, most of all. Some of my whippings were just macho show, but mostly they were pure logic. 7-16 looked at me and saw everything that their world said they were—soft and weak—and that could not be allowed. I didn't make many more friends on the Marshall Team that year. The few that I did could never understand why I would not fight.

I fit only slightly better back home. Our neighborhood was calm and could not compare with the rest of Mondawmin. We had only a smattering of Section 8, and no colorful legacy—no older gods regaled us with tales of knife fights and smack. All our houses were sedate and brick. They had bad self-esteem, were built on a natural incline, slumped down and into each other, had tiny backyards, basement doors embedded in the ground like bomb shelters. Insignificant lawns. Covered porches. But still, better—and yet worse than—the projects.

We had no rec centers or courts infested with ball hawks whose handles were legend. The courts at Druid Hill Park were beyond reach. I would launch kites from broad parking lots or get with Leroy and some friends to toss snowballs at buses and cabs. On the grass hill between Mondawmin and the crib, we drew up plays in our palms, hiked, and went deep. Behind our houses, we measured broad alleys and plotted courses for our Diamondback and Mongoose bicycles.

I had enough Knowledge to know that the athletes were our kings—Jordan, Tyson, and LT. And then there was Len Bias at the University of Maryland and his obnoxious array of shots. His game should have been locked in a cell. Bias had a first step that was unreal but was so complete that when everything pointed to a windmill or double pump, he'd pull up from eighteen feet and calmly shoot out the lights. Big Bill was entranced. He followed box scores in *The Sun*, cut out headlines, and fantasized about the Sweet 16.

Bill would ball up scrap paper in Dad's basement office and take aim at the trash can. He would bang and bend wire hangers until they rounded into a hoop and could be jammed between a door and the sill. Then he'd make a ball from the Sunday *Sun* and cover it with packing tape. His addiction was all consuming. He put me to work gathering Dad's tools, then boosting milk crates from the supermarket on the side of Mondawmin. In the alley between Forest Park and Liberty, Bill, Jay, Dante, and all the neighborhood boys convened. For Bill, turning an alley into a court was nothing—back in the projects he'd once conjured Madison Square Garden from a bicycle rim. He cut out the crate bottom, climbed a ladder while one of his boys held it secure, then nailed the makeshift goal to a backboard and phone pole. Then he grabbed the orange-striped rock, christened his creation with a short fadeaway and began chanting: Bias from eighteen feet, Bias coast to coast, Bias for the game.

The rules were organic. Breaks in the alley and cement were foul lines and boundaries. We were honorable and yelled "Ball!" when hacked. Starting with the rock, the alley flowered into a center of civilization. Bill would bring out his boom box and tapes of Frank Ski. Fools would pass

50

around air pistols and shoot the threading out of old ski jackets. It did not end in the winter. Clouds gathered and dumped snow over the city. But the next day, we'd be shoveling until we'd reclaimed a broad patch of gray. Then we'd go to war in our skullies. The crate would stand for months, until one morning we'd arrive and find only plastic bits and bent nails. I suspected ghosts, invoked by the new moon, rising up like Darryl Dawkins's revenge.

But I was still me and the alley was not my natural habitat. My default position was sprawled across the bed staring at the ceiling or cataloging an extensive collection of *X-Factor* comic books. This never cut it for Dad, who insisted I learn the wavelengths of my world. In the quiet chaos of my room, everything was certain. I'd be thumbing through the origin of Beast's feral blue coat or Jean Grey's telekinesis. And then my father would suddenly loom, a shadow in the doorway of my Eden.

Get outside, he'd tell me. This is your community. These are your people.

So I'd gather myself and meet Bill at the alley toting the world's ugliest game. I double dribbled, carried, hacked. My shot was swatted into gutters. I might get off two dribbles before the pickpockets went to work.

Back at home, Bill would catch me daydreaming and punch me in the arm, hoping I'd finally rise up and swing out of rage. But mostly I squealed and fell to the ground.

It was about that time that Bill started eyeing all of Tioga's honeys, scheming on ways to make me a man.

Yo, why don't you holler at Terra, Bill said, raising his eyes suggestively in the exaggerated way he borrowed from Ric Flair, a vestige of the boy still under his toughening skin, which made me groan. Shorty's phat to death.

Of course I'd noticed that all the girls around me had begun to hourglass. When I caught my first whiff of hair permed, pulled back, and tied with a red ribbon; of brown girls in teal dresses fluttering in the Sunday wind; of single mothers regal in Jordache, I thought of nothing else for days. There was too much of Dad in me, but never quite enough. I was debilitated by fear in the presence of girls, and that fear concealed a bedrock belief that I had nothing to offer or worthy to say.

So there was Terra, rocking the mushroom bob, her hips tapering down to her calves like the angles of an ice cream cone. She did not smile or laugh. She rarely talked and ran with older dudes, and this was horrifying. When in her area, my tongue swelled in my mouth. I went dumb and blind. I would slump my shoulders, stare at the ground, and wander home. Straight up the steps I'd flop on the bed and fall through sheets, box springs, and floors. Fall through green and gold leaves, until I arrived in a world where the rules were reworked. Terra floated across an ocean of pastel, until she stood before me, her lips parted with wanting. I reached out to close the distance, and the world shook and quaked. Big Bill was standing over me, punching me in the arm.

He must have taken all of this personally. He believed in the Coates's diaspora and his role as deputy patriarch. The kids were scattered across the area. Malik was out in East Baltimore. John in Randallstown. Kris and Kell off to the Mecca. But when we gathered under the roof of Tioga, Bill implanted himself on the throne. He would lead us to a matinee of *The Last Dragon* or keep score for a tournament of Summer Games. At night Tioga creaked and moaned. Bill would pass out hammers and joysticks to battle the burglars of imagination.

He assumed our weight, even if we didn't ask. I think it gave him a grander sense of self. But he was heir to even more than he could articulate. In those years, we looked at Dad, and misunderstood so much. On the side of my mother, we had cousins who were Americans. They cavorted out in suburban Columbia. They played Little League on sprawling well-funded fields. Their fathers were veterans, unbittered by Vietnam. They talked up barbecue, lug nuts, and golf. Their houses were detached. Their streets had names like Dove's Fly Way and Evergreen Road. They hung Christmas lights and had bathrooms where towels and washcloths matched. We were the same as them, and yet Dad had marooned us in this almost ghetto.

But Dad was unapologetic, and there were larger forces in play. Here we were in the throes of a second *Maafa*—or maybe an extension of the first. All around us the old order of black fathers was tilting toward disgrace, trading in their honor for wine and dice, and leaving in their wake legions of boys, dizzied, angry, and confused. But Dad resisted the heathen call, parted the stagnant lake of fallen knights, and reached for his blade.

To be Conscious Man was more than just the digestion of obscure books that happen to favor your side. It was a feeling, an ingrained sense that something major in our lives had gone wrong. My father was haunted. He was bad at conjuring small talk, he watched very little TV, because once Conscious, every commercial, every program must be strip-mined for its deeper meaning, until it lays bare its role in this sinister American plot.

He was not humorless. One winter he tossed out our green couch and didn't buy another one for four years. Bill would fume over the lack of furniture, but when friends and family would come past, Dad would look over the empty space and say, Oh hey, Gary, have a seat on our new couch, man. It's leather.

Some Sundays he'd watch football with me, the two of

us lying on that empty stretch of floor. He'd cheer for the Eagles as they whipped on my beloved Dallas Cowboys and I'd switch sides.

Son, you aren't a real fan if you switch.

But even here he was not free. In the days when there were no other black quarterbacks, he loved Doug Williams, rooted for him in Tampa Bay. Then in the winter of 1987, Williams, now with the Redskins, came hobbling off the bench in the Super Bowl and my father stood in front of the TV shaking his fist, yelling Go, Dougie, go! Williams smoked Denver for all of us—four touchdowns in one quarter—and became the first brother to raise the Lombardi Trophy. Dad glowed when Williams' dark hands wrapped themselves around the prize. And Dad didn't even like the Redskins.

But he looked at everything through the lens of his people. He'd read the prophecy of Marcus Garvey—and my father believed. Dad took up that call, the charge to make Garvey's kingdom real, and to us, he was unbreakable.

But he was also unbearable. In the late '70s my parents bought a house on Woodbrook Avenue. In 1979, my father went away to Atlanta University for grad school in library science. My mother, barely thirty, would sit on the bed and cry.

Dad was working on his own version of *halaal*. He

was always dangerous when given too much time to think. At varying points he banned white flour, white rice, sugar, and all meat. Before, he'd made ice cream and cookies adorned with peaches. Our treats were raisins and peanuts and carob brownies. He served whole-wheat pancakes with honey. Fish became the family treat. But I was allergic and would break out in hives if they brought too much of it in the house. By the time we moved to Tioga, Dad had loosened up, forced into compromise by the practicalities. Sugar and poultry were back. Ma would bake carrot cake from scratch and barbecue chicken legs.

But when Bill moved back in with us, he was used to steak, ribs, sausage—the regular fare when he lived with his mom. Once he looked on as Ma prepared a pack of Leanies—hot dogs engineered for vegetarians.

This isn't a hot dog, he helpfully pointed out to my mother.

In this house, it is, she replied. You want something different, go buy it yourself.

Bill and Ma had all the distance you could imagine. She was his stepmother, but that sort of technical phrasing—along with half brother, and half sister—was never allowed in my house. Still, Bill was a loyalist to the core. Dad would leave the crib for days, off to do the math on a forgotten historian, track down the copyright for a book, or persuade someone to donate their papers to the Mecca. Dad was great about the grand vision, but he often left details to others; and while Bill lived on Tioga, my mother often had to work to keep him in check.

At Tioga, Ma did the legwork and caught the blowback. When it came to the day-to-day discipline, Dad was a worst-case scenario, summoned when we'd gone too far. In those moments, Ma would cock her head and walk away. It was left to us to wait in our bedrooms, until late night or early morning, when the wraith got to swinging his black belt.

We had to do something ignorant for that, a feat I managed annually. But Ma was hard core in her own right, and most dangerous when she lowered her voice slightly a few decibels above a whisper. She was raised in the projects down on Gilmore, and as a girl, never saw a fight she didn't want. Dad generated a fear that was supernatural, but my mother was his earthly, overseeing manifestation. I was closer to my mother in those days, mostly because while Dad lectured from Olympus and could descend like a plague, she talked easily and discussed everything like it was a local weather report, even sex.

Now, boy, she once told me, in one of her many renditions of the Talk. Whenever you start, be gentle. Don't get there and start jumping up and down on the girl. Remember to be gentle.

But she didn't protect us from Dad, and in his stead,

she could be ruthless. My mother delivered my first beatings. Once while I was mouthing off, she reached for a high heel. I took off running, and then felt the sudden impulse to dodge to the right. The shoe whizzed past me and smashed a dent into the wall. I turned around in shock. Ma laughed and walked away.

Bill resented the awkward relationship between my mother and him. Once, I came home and caught him in full rage. He was on the phone with a friend. He threatened to pull tool on Dad. He called my mother—with her short, Conscious natural hair—a bald-headed bitch. I walked past him quickly and didn't say anything. I was never comfortable with anger. I would feel the claws of rage digging into me, but my nature never allowed them to hang on for long. I thought that the rage just went away. It took years to find out I was wrong. But back then, I did not know where to go.

I didn't say much to him for the next week. I knew the rules about insulting mothers, the obligations of the son. I should have been thinking of arsenic-laced cookies, a hot poker in the eyes while he slept. But I was bad at holding on to the dark burn that feeds revenge. Instead, I almost understood. We were of different mothers, what we saw in the world was not the same. He was a terrible bear, but still I held Bill in that place that most young boys hold their heroic brothers. I pilfered his old Nike tees, and gray Adidas sweat suits in hopes that all his heart, his stones, his terrifying bop had seeped through in the wash and would now react with something latent and manly in me.

That was, of course, fantastic folly. Back at school, I marveled as my man Fruitie went from herb to culture hero. We were down by law, both awkward and out of sorts with the Lemmel ecology. His handle on the rock was questionable. His choice of fashion was pedestrian. He had the sort of easy temperament that most of the other boys tried to cover with armor. His slave name was Antwan Smith, but the Marshall Team addressed him as Fruitie because he laughed at anything, told bad jokes, and cared nothing for the mask and shadows seemingly necessitated by the street. Like me, he had some height on him and came from one of those nameless places that the goblins did not fear. But that was where our parallels reached a dead end.

I lost count of how many times Fruitie got banked. The accounts came back as oral history with variations on the same heroic theme: There Fruitie stood at the base of the school steps, surrounded by vandals who dared not shoot the fair one, even though Fruitie was chill and always at ease. Instead, they circled, looking for the perfect angle to sucker punch. Niggers never even saw Fruitie's ax, only the surge of boys flinging themselves at him and then flying away, no longer under their own power. He fought fiercely, repelled waves, before going down. With each telling, the deeds became greater, the villainy swelled in number, their methods grew in atrocity. They came from Douglass High School, damn near grown men. They lumbered out of the woods by the score. They pulled up in paint-splattered work vans. They wore hard hats and steel-toe boots. They swung two-by-fours, pipes, and brickbats. Not once did Fruitie prevail, and yet for the sheer will to war, he was John Henryed and the Marshall Team conferred on him a sort of respect that no jump shot or dime piece could give. The Gods of the Avenue mocked him. The time and the era outmatched him. But he would not be contained.

Out on the bus stop, where Garrison and Liberty meet, he revealed the source of his power while I stared on, unbelieving. We were catty-corner from a fire station and across the street from Jim Parker Lounge. I was shivering in the winter, having just had my sky blue Nike skullcap snatched.

This is the sort of dumb shit that slowly takes us out. There existed a Baltimore where school is for school's sake, where a kid's greatest worries were spelling tests and the first awkward juvenile crush. Neighborhoods like Rolling Park had bullies, fat kids, and badasses in a rebellious phase.

But in Mondawmin the vultures among us corrupted everything. They were not growing into something better; they were not finding their deeper selves. The Knowledge was a disease. Some took to it faster than others. But eventually we all got it. We all grew tired of getting touched. We were just like boys everywhere, dreaming of model trains, Captain Marvel, and chemistry sets. But for us there were orcs outside the door, blood in their teeth and always waiting. At some point we grew tired of crumbling under their boots and embraced the Knowledge, became like all the rest groping for manhood in the dark.

Each black boy must find his own way to this understanding. Fruitie was a blue jay in the meadow, and that made him remarkable, because even he had come to Know. That winter afternoon, while the vultures swooped in and took off with my hat, all I had to do was whistle and Fruitie would have been at them. But I did nothing. After the spot rushers had gone, Fruitie stepped into the awkward air and dropped a jewel. He confessed to me that he was afraid, but when surrounded by henchmen, he'd quote a line from Rakim Allah and he was harder than he'd been in the moment before.

I nodded, but pushed his words into the back of a basement. Some weeks later, on the field across from Lemmel, we were shortcutting to the M-1 bus stop—he was headed home, I was off to see my grandmother. And then here these mutherfuckers came, with more numbers than us, running across the field between west of Dukeland and south of Liberty. I've forgotten how they looked on purpose, but I remember that again they grabbed for my Raiders fitted, yet another hat, and then snatched something from Fruitie that I didn't see. They offered to let us go with no further damage. I accepted. But Fruitie had grown tired long ago. There is no other way to say this: I walked away.

From the safety of the bus stop I watched him. He was not Thor. When he swung his long arms, nothing shook on its axis. Within seconds he was on the ground. It was horror. They were on top of him, wailing away. Fruitie was gone. He thrashed wildly, kicked his legs. How could this sight, him helpless on the ground, pinned in a one on six be poetry? I was a boy like all boys, selfish in my own particular way. What I could not understand was something that seemed elemental to everyone else around me—that a kid who lost his heart was worthy of nothing.

The next day at school, the whole affair, like always, had gone around the Marshall Team. Someone approached me in science class—

Fruitie should fuck you up.

But that was never my nigger's style. He gave a pound when he saw me, and kept joking like nothing had happened, like nothing had gone wrong. His kindness wounded me. And I knew then that I was alone.

CHAPTER 3

Africa's in the house, they get petrified

My father was not a violent man. He went organic in the '70s, before Whole Foods became fashion, and kept a vegetable garden in our small backyard. I never saw him argue in public. I never saw him hit anyone but his kids. He kept one gun in the house. It was a relic—a broken rifle from his Panther days, stowed at the bottom of our coat closet beneath old jackets and desert boots. He loved foreign movies, and would make a weekly hajj to the artsy Charles Theater downtown for a taste of Truffaut. But his aspect deflected the shuck and jive, and he believed in man's inescapable lower nature.

He took a broad view of scholarship, and expected that I'd leave junior high with the rudiments of manhood. He was like all parents, urging for the grades that he believed matched my potential. But more so, he expected I'd leave Lemmel with Knowledge, Consciousness, and the sense to deploy each in its appropriate place. Dad had seen more than just the streets by then, and at every station he noted the people who staked their lives on turning you to their ends. Today, he told me, it was wild boys in search of skullies, later it'd be a girlfriend subbing you in for her no-shit father or supervisors who pushed you into taking their weight. The Knowledge Rule 2080: From maggots to men, the world is a corner bully. Better you knuckle up and go for yours than have to bow your head and tuck your chain.

Dad wanted me present to everything, my entire neurology cocked. But I sleepwalked through the world, hoping one day to wake up on a fantastic other side and realize that this had all been a dream. I was clueless to more than just the street shit—I was the type of child who lost his hats and jackets on the first warm day of the year. Dad would lecture, and the words would fly straight past. It was like I heard them but could not translate.

When I turned nine, I got my first set of house keys, and lost them an average of once a month. This was heresy and Dad's warnings stretched into double digits, until follow-through was all that was left.

Where're your keys? he demanded.
I don't have them, I mumbled.

He was standing in the living room, off from work, always off from work at the most awful times. House keys seem small, but to my father they embodied everything about me that could someday get me killed.

Well, where are they?
This kid at school took them from me and threw them in the trash.
Did you pull them out?
No.
Did you pop the kid in the mouth?
No.
What did you do?
Nothing.

This is when Dad snapped. There was some calculation and illusion here. Dad wasn't the type to have a bad day at work and come home and start swinging. Equally, there would be days when the teacher called home and you were certain a beating was on the way, and he would sit at the table and talk. But this made it worse, because when we were wrong, we felt trapped in a horror movie. We never knew what was coming, how it was coming, or when.

Dad walked up the steps and came back with his black leather belt, folded so that the buckle met the tip. He jabbed me in the chest and asked who I was more scared of—him or them.

I bring this here to intimidate, he said. To show you what I am. To show you that I mean business. But this isn't what it's about anymore.

Then he dropped the belt on the brown carpet and started swinging.

My father fought his whole life, but once he'd been like me—from the street but not of it. He was indoctrinated at eight. Dad lived with his tangled family on Markoe Street in West Philadelphia. His father had kids by three sisters, so that Aunt Pearl, who Dad loved, defied classification, and his four brothers and sisters were also cousins. My grandfather was in his late forties, and winding down his reign as the satyr king of North Philly. He was profligate, and seemed to reveal new children the way others revealed ordinary vases, penny loafers, and belt buckles. He was pretty—tall, light, and did not need stocking caps, hot water, and Murray's grease for waves. He loved the newspaper, and it fell on my father to feed this daily hunger. He did this faithfully until one evening, he returned holding nothing, crying about kids on the corner who'd roughed him up.

Go get my paper, my grandfather told him. If you come back without it, you'll have to fight me.

Dad protested.

Son, he told him, the first one who says something, you pop him in the mouth and try to kill him. You do that and I promise you'll have my paper.

This is one of those stories where the feeling of the moment stands in for visual detail. In Dad's telling the fight is two shadows rolling around, but what is solid is the feeling, not of explicit triumph but of an awkward victory—the win that does not come from vanquishing a foe but fear. Conjuring the will to campaign. Now he was armed with that magic, that first taste of freedom earned, and he knew he could walk his block as he pleased, could buy his father's paper at midnight under a starless sky, if that's what he wanted. Predators would never see him as easy, because he'd reached out and tapped into the great forces that ward the vultures away. That Knowledge was for beyond Markoe Street. Years later, these same kids would be adults, subtle and dignified. But Dad could see their beaks, red eyes, and battered black wings.

Still even then he was Dad, not meant to make a life on the block. He had no real swagger or pose. He was an incompetent thug, the sort of boy who knew how to keep the heat off but not how to bring it. He got caught stealing and throwing bottles at white boys. He dropped out of school, bragged that there was nothing there for him to learn. He haunted libraries at odd hours in search of more Mickey Spillane. You could have asked him what he wanted to be back then, and though he could not name it, he would have told you about the trips downtown, how'd he run his hand across the base of tall buildings that he was sure he would one day own.

Dad was of that era, an acolyte of that peculiar black faith that makes us patriots despite the yoke. So he worshipped JFK, got amped off old war movies, dreamed of leaping over sand hills, driving tanks, and tossing grenades. He was semi-Conscious then. He worked delivering groceries for A&P on Broad Street, a few doors down from the Uptown. Next door was the state liquor store and on the second floor a Nation of Islam mosque. He saw Malcolm in the flesh, and noted with interest the nationalists out on Columbia Avenue and their posters of noble Ethiopians, the ones who would not beg. Martin Luther King was just beginning his tour of the South. Dad had never seen a water fountain or toilet reserved by race, and could not access the Other Knowledge that called on young men to sing while barbarians swung clubs and unleashed dogs.

There were few options in his vicinity, no collegiates on his block, and whenever he strayed from his own street the reception he got was Hey, mutherfucker, where you from? So he fell back on his dreams of John Wayne. In the army, he handled dogs for the military police, was shipped to Vietnam with only the vaguest sense of its place in politics or history. He was the only brother in his unit. It was like anything else—some of the white boys were human, but others ran cock block between Dad and the Vietnamese girls. When he busted out his battery-powered record player and threw on the latest Stax, they'd howl and laugh. While on leave he concocted payback, bought an armful of Dylan records, knowing only that Dylan sounded hillbilly.

In the tent he shared with his unit, he played "Masters of War," and mocked them, but more mocked himself. They loved Dylan like Dad loved Pat Boone, which is to say not at all. But his image of whiteness was so flat that he assumed they all banged to the same soulless beat. Then the plot inverted. Dylan's voice was awful, an aged quaver that sounded nothing like the deep-throated or silky R&B that Dad took as gospel. But the lyrics wore him down, until he played Dylan in that addicted manner of college kids who cordon off portions of their lives to decipher the prophecies of their favorite band. Dad heard poetry, but more than that an angle that confirmed what a latent part of him had already suspected. This war was bullshit.

Even then, in his army days, Dad was more aware than most. Back in training he'd scuffled with a Native American soldier, who tried to better his social standing by airing out the unit's only black. After they were pulled apart, Dad walked up to his room, calmed down, and then returned to the common area. On a small table, he saw a copy of *Black Boy*. He just knew someone was fucking with him. But he picked up the book, and discerned that it was Nobody Smiling. He took it up to his room, mostly because he was touched but also to keep the book from playing a part in any further racist slights.

In Richard Wright, Dad found a literature of himself. He'd read *Manchild in the Promised Land* and *Another Country*, but from Wright he learned that there was an entire shadow canon, a tradition of writers who grabbed the pen, not out of leisure but to break the chain. He bubbled on the edge of Consciousness. The night they gunned Malcolm down, Dad and a few black soldiers were headed into town to carouse and drink. The message came over the radio, but the rest of the car kept talking.

Quiet, Dad told them. Did you hear what they just said? Malcolm is dead. There were a few looks of shallow concern and then the conversation picked up, like only a strong wind had interrupted the flow.

Now he began to come to. When on leave, he stopped at book stands in search of anything referencing his own. He read Malcolm's memoir, and again saw some of his own struggle, and now began to feel things he'd, like us all, long repressed—the subtle, prodding sense that he was seen as less. He went back to Baldwin, who posed the great paradox that would haunt him to the end: Who among us would integrate into a burning house?

He was discharged in 1967 and married Linda, in love, but mostly because he knew nothing else. It was wrong from the moment they left the courthouse. Afterward, they gathered with Dad's family to talk, laugh, and drink. Halfway through the day Linda left the small party, and said she was just stepping out to visit her mother. But she never came back, and Dad spent that evening at Ms. Verla's house pleading for his new wife's return. She did, but they argued regularly. They'd take turns leaving and coming, and during periods of intermittent warmth, children would appear.

By the time the second child arrived, my big sister Kris, six years my senior, he was in bloom. You know one way or the other we all get touched. A Jersey housewife strolls through the supermarket and, suddenly caught by the sheen of an apple, decides to give abortions in small-town Kansas. A washed-up middling exec, who's thrown his life away to the bottle, hears organs, finds the Word. In the midst of a Hawthorne lecture, a drug-addled sophomore is taken by dreams of the Peace Corps. All the truly living, at least once, are born again.

Since childhood, Dad had read constantly but without direction or edge. Baldwin, Wright, and Malcolm were the first signs that led him onto another path, one he followed until enveloped by a forest of black books. He lived in a busy house, but in stolen moments alone he considered the world around him, the quaking from war, riots, and assassinations, and saw in this new Knowledge a way of drawing a line.

When the years of slumber passed, and he emerged fully Conscious, everything was skewed. Was like the whole world needed a shot of V8. Where others saw America in lovely columns, marvels of engineering, and refined democrats, Dad saw only masks concealing the heralds of woe. He was a slave still, and all around him black people heaved under the invisible yoke. He could not talk like before. Everything felt corrupted, until he found himself sitting at cookouts, wondering how, in the world of Medgar Evers, a man could sidle up, crack a beer, and spend hours essaying on Earl Weaver and the Oriole way.

Dad was working for United Airlines, unloading luggage and maintaining the cabin after passengers deplaned. In downtime, he brought back his father's old ritual and fell into the newspapers left behind from distant cities and states. He only barely knew California, but it was in a story from that other country that Dad found his muse. His muse carried a gun.

Television remembers that era for the blown churches, Mississippi savages, and sharecroppers gone philosophical. All those great stories are Southern and built on Christ. But Dad wasn't from those parts. He hailed from the black metropolis, walked with the great black masses, down on the Markoe Streets of the world, where we had all been down so long. He stood with those who had come to believe that our condition, the worst of this country's condition—poor, diseased, illiterate, crippled, dumb—was not just a tumor to be burrowed out but proof that this whole body was a tumor, that America was not a victim of great rot but rot itself. Dad found Gandhi absurd. Much more native to Dad were these fab headlines touting the exploits of the brothers and sisters from Oakland who did not dance, who preached righteous self-defense and Fanon.

Word to John Brown, my father was overcome. It was

the spring of 1969. He began checking the schedule for planes coming from the West Coast. On board, after cleaning, he now searched for California papers, then searched through those papers for any updates on the machinations and movements of the Panther Party. He finally discovered the local Panthers after a night of cocktails with a girl who was not Linda but claimed to be down and, as proof, that very night, pointed Dad to the local office.

The next day, he arrived at the branch cocked and ready to serve. But the Panthers were in the throes of Hoover's scripted paranoia. Everyone was a presumed agent. Members were purged. This was not a game. Alleged informants were found decomposing in the woods of Leakin Park. When Dad walked in, dripping revolutionary fervor, they held back. They wanted to know how he found them. They did not recognize the girl who pointed him their way.

He was assigned to a weekly political education class—a sort of vetting that weeded out the agents and crazies who did not so much believe in dialectical materialism and great leaps forward as in the sheen of guns and shooting at cops. It was supposed to be about more than that, which suited Dad's bearing and penchant for books more than guns. He would listen to the autodidacts break down capitalism and the means of production. He would listen to them turn around the great conflicts many ways, and he would say nothing; until one day he saw a clear through line, then they could not shut him up. They could not turn him away.

There were no berets and powder-blue shirts. Often there weren't even guns. Dad began as the Panther who wasn't. He was designated a "community worker"—a tag ranking him slightly above hanger-on and giving him sleeping rights at the collective's HQ. He would rise at five A.M., head over to the Martin de Porres Center, talk with the radical Catholics, and then head to the kitchen. The revolution was centered around pancakes, bacon, and grits; and by seven A.M., a stream of poor black kids would move through for their daily free meal. In the afternoons, he studied with his comrades. At night he worked at the airport. Somewhere in between he was a father.

This creaky arrangement held until he was busted for moving guns. He lost his job. The newspapers published his name and address. He called Linda, and she just hung up the phone. The dead connection broke his bonds to the mortal plane. He saw himself now freed from this world and all its trappings, which would soon be nil anyway. He went to work full-time for the uprising, and found his place among the great change that was burning through the city.

Dad rose through the ranks that had been thinned by arrests, underground escapes, and stupidity. He was the Maryland defense captain, head of the Baltimore branch.

But he planned no insurrections and avoided the grand suicidal gesture that seduced others of his age. Instead, Dad mostly thought of survival. For sure, there was the threat of cops kicking down doors, infiltration by agents and operatives. But these were secondary. Dad was responsible for a commune, and when he woke in the morning he thought not of guns but of oil, electricity, water, rent, and groceries. He turned to Brother Reginald Howard, his minister of distribution and right-hand man who worked down at Bethlehem Steel.

Howard, Dad would say, we don't have any money.

Formally, Howard's charge was the delivery and flow of Panther newspapers, the funds from which were the lifeblood of any Panther chapter. He was a hustler in the righteous sense, the type who sold Panther newspapers at that plant between shifts. Dad would send him out into the street and Howard would speak with local grocers, highlighting all the kids the Panthers had fed, all the free shoes they'd handed out, and the mothers they'd tested for sickle cell.

Then there was the plight of the community. They would start to roll in early, drawn by the luster of the party or referred by some overwhelmed city agency, and all of them needed help. Someone got harassed by white people in East Baltimore. A husband arrested and couldn't afford a lawyer. Someone else had been evicted and sat out.

And then there was the struggle of managing the soldiers of the impending guerrilla war. Dad was not in the company of flower power. It took all kinds, bourgeois college students, teenage mothers, plumbers, and professors. But the beloved and honored foot soldiers hailed from the back end of the world. They were risen armies of the dead—cutthroats, rapists, brigands, and murderers—who in other lives feasted on their own people's toil. Now they'd gone Conscious and trained their guns on the System. But the reformation varied in scope. Some were as real as Malcolm straight out the joint, while others were just looking for new ways to launder their dirt.

Back in Washington, Hoover was wild and aflame. Later it all came out—reams of FBI files where agents fomented beef, trumped up charges, and coaxed the vanguard to suicidal acts. The Panthers needed only their eyes to understand. Across the country, police armed with blueprints and intelligence above their grade kicked in doors at perfect hours. They murdered Fred Hampton. Bound and gagged Bobby Seale. Eldridge was out. Attica and the Jackson brothers were on the way.

In Baltimore it went like anywhere else, and among the matters my father inherited in his new role were the numerous cases of shackled Panthers. He focused on Eddie Conway, indicted for the murder of a policeman. He was pinned by the slimmest of evidence—a jailhouse snitch and an officer who claimed to have seen his face for a few seconds in the dead of night. But the Panther leaders were only half concerned with the particulars. The romance of the movement, the theology of revolution tomorrow, made them see not one man in the balance but a symbol of the grander war.

The leadership sent orders to Dad. Conway was to boycott the trial and expose this rotting system of justice, from the pigs to the preening judge, for the bane that it was. They placed their faith in the jury, convinced that they, too, would see the sin of it all. But the Panthers' faith exceeded their resolve, and all the talk drove them to delusion. Brothers out west promised big-shot lawyers—Charles Garry and William Kunstler. Instead, Conway got a public defender who spent all of an hour with him before the trial. In the end Conway—Brother Eddie as I came to know him—went to jail for life plus thirty-seven years and, of the many things from this time which Dad would have to carry on his conscience, that was king.

Across the nation Panthers shouldered the burdens of their comrades and the community. It was what they'd asked for. And then, in 1972, they were ordered to stop. It fell apart on bullshit rhetorical points, a game of who was really ready to go for the guns. Eldridge Cleaver allied with the New York branch, and after that it was gang war.

Panthers killing each other. First the rebel Robert Webb, then party loyalist Sam Napier was found bound, gagged, burned, and shot in New York. Only weeks earlier he'd been with my father, and they'd narrowly escaped the justice of the New York faction. Dad was summoned to the headquarters in California and has remained puzzled by what he saw ever since. It was about that time it dawned on him: the world was going to go on as it was.

In California, the higher-ups informed him that Oakland was the only front that mattered, that beefs with local liquor stores were the real makings of this new world. They shut down all the regional offices, and Dad was left to stew on the many Eddie Conways, Panthers who had acted in this theater, now left in jail. Then there were the communities, where Panthers provided shoes, doctors, breakfast, and lawyers, abandoned and left to their squalor. And Dad had his own kids, now, five of them, back in Baltimore with a father away on the other side. This was too much for Dad to take. He was identified as a noncompliant and put under house arrest by the Panther Party. He scrounged together money from family and friends and flew back home.

It could've been worse. Whatever he faced—pissed-off mothers and grandparents, old taxes and new debt—was nothing like the chasm that swallowed others. Dad believed in revolution, but the truth is, he was always eminently suitable to the world as it was. He was an intellectual, born as it happened among people who could not see a college campus as an outcome.

He thought his country rotten, but he was a better fit than he knew. His comrades were ill equipped. This was about more than shackles of color. They flocked to their revolution because the real revolution, the one that won out—with its marching automation, its theology of efficiency and goods—had nothing for them. A radical undoing was their only way out. Behold how they died: scrounging for crack rocks; infested by AIDS; or, if lucky, under the honorable hail of gunfire.

I begin many years later, After the Fall, after the terrible dawning that the revolution had gone bacchanal, and devolved into shakedowns of drug dealers and parlor games with starlets and playboys who longed to look like danger. Dad and many of his Baltimore comrades had left the Panthers. The final hours of their youth were heartbreaking. They picketed liquor stores for donations, shook cups in Berkeley next to the white homeless, and financed a nightclub. For leaving, the Panthers condemned my father. They instructed Patsy to not allow Dad to see Johnathan. Dad wrote a letter to the central committee. There was no answer.

He was caught somewhere between the old socialism and the understanding that the people could not be moved

without capital. Still, he left the Panthers with a basic belief system, a religion that he would pass on to his kids. He
jettisoned Christmas and saw the great apostasy of the
Fourth of July. He took a pact with a group of brothers and
sisters to fast on Thanksgiving in protest over Attica, the
Indians, and the sheer gluttony of Satan. Through the
years, these brothers fell away. But Dad carried on.

Now he thought back to the Panthers' heyday and his
old friend Walter Lively, who like him, was young, black,
and out of Philly. But Lively had an instinct for the inside,
and was thus adept at moving the gears of power in the
proper direction. He was a shocking blizzard of things. He
was named to the city council at twenty-five as a Republi-
can. Finagled a farm in rural Pennsylvania where Dad
would stash Panthers on the run. But what struck Dad
the most was Walter Lively's dream of a propaganda machine—a vertically integrated entity that printed, published, and distributed Consciousness to the people. Lively
had assembled many pieces of printing equipment, but before bringing it to be, he was on to something else.

Dad picked up the idea. He thought back to the Panthers and their study of Kim II Sung and his parable of the
One Hero. It was said that when the Japanese invaded, all
the men reached for their guns, but the One Hero grabbed
a mimeograph machine. A bullet could fell one enemy, a
grenade a few more, but the mimeograph could kill the

hearts and minds of thousands and resurrect many more of your own. Dad conceived a new revolution in Lively's three parts—a bookstore, a printer, and a publisher—that would give the people control of information.

He convened many disaffected revolutionaries. They were a mix of cultural nationalists, militant unionists, and draft resisters straight out of the brig. They did not cohere. They fought over intercommunalism and dialectics. They fought over the working class and the precise calibrations of the petit bourgeoisie. They split and went their separate ways. Dad and Brother Howard, his comrade from the Panther days, carried on. They moved forward with their plans for a propaganda machine, called it the George Jackson Movement. Its namesake was the incarcerated scholar and Black Panther, who predicted ghettos surrounded by barbwire, grenade launchers smuggled into Watts. Jackson took Angela Davis as a spiritual lover, published two books mulling the coming rebellion, and was martyred in San Quentin, after supposedly having concealed a pistol in his Afro. The George Jackson Movement acquired a storefront on Pennsylvania Avenue. Dad and Brother Howard painted and did repairs. They threw a cabaret, played music, served food, and took donations of books, which became the first seeds of a bookstore. They mailed some of these books to the brothers in prison. Some of the brothers traded the books for cigarettes.

It is now 1973. My mother is living with Grandma on Penhurst Avenue. Grandma had come up from the Eastern Shore, endured a broken marriage, raised kids in the projects, and now owned her own home. My mother was her last daughter. She was just out of college, teaching school in Baltimore, and on her way, like her sisters, into the soft, safe arms of the middle class. Had it gone the way it should have, my name might be Otha or Ray. I might have played soccer, worshipped Christmas, joined the Scouts. Ma was from a righteous old-school black family. They believed in the supremacy of God and country and the grand power of hard work. My father was not a detour, was not a hard right but a parallel universe—Stormshadow and Spirit—where each one of those values was worshipped to a different end.

But my mother was done different. She was one of three sisters. The oldest, Ava, was dubbed the smart one. The middle girl, Jo-Ann, was brown and lovely. Ma scrounged for her place. She was skinny. She wore Coke bottle glasses. She had bad hair and a gap between her teeth. She failed third grade and did not learn to read until she was nine. Around the way, kids teased her and laughed. She was slow with her words and quick with her fists. She was the sort of girl whose aunts told her that personality would take her a long way. There was truth there. She was tough but magnetic, lived to entertain and make family and friends laugh. She was a lovely dancer—once stood in her uncle Otha's record shop with a Dreamsicle and did the twist until the ice cream shot off the stick and flew away.

She grew up around her own. White people were absent, theoretical, and subject to unsubstantiated conjecture. She remembers the assassination of Martin Luther King most clearly because the rioting interrupted her senior prom. Still, there was that same vague sense that something was wrong, and in her already alienation, she felt that gnaw. She went natural in high school, and only permed her hair again for her sister's wedding after Grandma threatened to leave her out. At college, she was arrested for protesting. She hung posters of the Panthers in her dorm room.

She briefly met Dad once, after she donated to the Panthers' free clothing program. And then again when her best friend suggested they visit the George Jackson Prison Movement. She was one of many who came there to study various books. Dad made an unromantic impression. He wore cheap clothes. His hair rebelled against combs. He had five kids, who at any moment could be roaming about the bookstore. He wore old shoes. He lived with various women. But he was all brainpower. He had dropped out of high school but could think in ways that the credentialed class could not conceive. He helped my mother get an A on her senior thesis. He preached about the people's need for

books, and he provided them. He organized social activities—celebrations of the family or children's books. His
kids were always with him. His various lovers were put
to work.

By now, Linda had thrown him out. He erected a par-
tition in the back of the Jackson Movement's headquarters
and lived in this makeshift half-room for many months. Ma
would come to the festivals and discussions, and then tease
him for being homeless. At the time she was in love with
an ex-con. She gave this man an autographed copy of *Black
Man of the Nile,* one of the texts Dad had prescribed. The
book had no effect, and instead of grabbing the mantle of
his ancestors, Ma's paramour robbed a church. Ma was carrying his baby. He called her—

Cheryl, the money is hidden in my apartment, in my
bedroom. Please take it to my lawyer.

Ma went and got the cash, took what she needed for
an abortion, and gave the rest to his lawyer. She did not answer any more of his calls.

When she returned to the bookstore, she was solo. She
had graduated from college, now teaching. She bought an
orange Volkswagen bug.

Dad: When do I get to ride in your car?
Ma: Let's go.

Dad was ill acquainted with the social intricacies of courting. No woman affiliated with him can remember anything resembling a date. He was not cheap or dispassionate as much as he was uncouth and all about business. Even among the Conscious brothers he was different. He seldom wore dashikis. His Afro was negligible. He would not light the candles of Kwanzaa. He was a world my mother had not seen. He cooked beans without meat. He bought fried fish from Ray's Seafood near North and Smallwood and poured on hot sauce until she cried. After hours, she would stop by and find Dad in the back with brother Howard tackling a pint of Jack.

He chafed at the thought of more kids. But when my mother saw him, she thought of redemption. Whenever he appeared, Bill, Kelly, Malik, or some other child was hanging on his neck, and he was so in love with them all. They were out driving to anyone knows where. She was firm and direct. Dad pulled the Volkswagen bug over to the side of the road.

Dad: Cheryl, I can't have more kids. I have five. I can barely provide for the ones I have.

Ma: You have five, but I have none. And I don't need you to provide—I can do that on my own. What I need is someone to be a man, and I think you're a wonderful father. I think you are raising beautiful kids.

Dad's ego swelled all over him. It was the winter of '74. I was born in the fall of '75. My father was twenty-nine. My mother was twenty-four. Dad had evolved and was present for my birth. I was brought home to a broken row house on Park Heights Avenue. Rats sped down the storm drain. They moved further down Park Heights. The weekly rent was $41, and it was the hardest money Dad ever had to earn in his life.

The life of a revolutionary was not paying off. He was conned into becoming a better man. The VA promised checks in compensation for each of his kids, if he would go back to school. He enrolled at Antioch College with no plans for graduation, strictly in it for the checks. And then he watched as brothers who came after him left before. He was thirty, an age he never expected to reach, and he began to comprehend the need for some sort of plan.

When I was three, he got his BA, then shipped off to Atlanta University for a master's. He came back and took his first professional job sorting histories for the official library of the Mecca. By then, he boiled down his dream of vertical integration to the step that fascinated him most. He'd begun publishing just before he left for Atlanta. Now he plumbed through all the old works by black scholars, works lost to time, and brought them back, restored in all their splendor.

Among the Conscious, a man is only worth his latest reading. Each page pulled you farther out of slumber, and among the most enlightened it was not uncommon to hear an entire conversation composed of footnotes.

In his bookstore days, Dad would sit behind the counter, nodding his way through the zealous interrogation of a new convert, who had nothing better to do than go to school.

Conscious: You read J. A. Rogers's "Hitler and the Negro"? Do you carry *100 Amazing Facts*?

Dad: It's in the back.

Conscious: Yeah, I see you got that. But what about *As Nature Leads*?

Dad: We don't carry either.

Conscious: See, that's the problem with black bookstores. Can't have enough J. A., brother.

Dad: Right, right. Mmmhmm.

Conscious: See, brother, those books are out of print. You know what that means? The white man ain't gonna let you see those. He don't want those books in print.

But Dad was not half stepping. And where others talked and complained, he journeyed through the library stacks, found a trove of books and pamphlets that expressed the world from our angle. Then he followed the notes from these books until he was enmeshed in a forgotten world of black literature and scholarship. The titles ran the gamut from lynching to ancient Ethiopia to the memoirs of cowboy Nat Love.

He began in the basement of our Park Heights row house, with a tabletop offset printer and four out-of-print pamphlets brought back from the edge. It was 1978, and this was a different magic. The Panthers were a sweeping romance—the young promise of shooting and fucking your way out of Donna Reed and into Pam Grier. But when Dad went to publishing, he scaled back into matrimony and left the world of mass upheaval. History would be altered, not in the swoop but with the long slow reawakening.

In my early years, I only barely understood how different my family was. When I was six we moved to a lovely house on Barrington Road. Our neighborhood was an island in the sky. There were windows everywhere, each with a different, awesome view of the world. A broad wooden porch extended from the front door and around to the side, until it formed a large L. When it rained, I'd sit outside listening to thunder, counting the seconds between sound and light. In the attic, I threaded trains and tracks through green foam mountains and imagined stops in sleepy towns far to the north.

I was down with my brother Malik. With three years between us, and a shared interest in alternative reality, I was closest to him in age and disposition. On weekends, we would sprawl across the living room floor in front of the wood-burning stove, and go rooting through the Isle of Dread or In Search of the Unknown. When I held polyhedral dice, their many sides were all futures, shards of other worlds where Medusae flashed their dead gazes and my dwarven thrower shattered against stone. I was young, chubby, and still completely smiles. My skin was clear and brown. My eyes were wide like my name. My styleless haircut was the work of my father, my widow's peak crawling out like a spy. Life was as open and possible as those emerald dice from Geppi's.

Ma would say that one day I would fly. She did not know. On the living room floor I had papers spread in front of me, with wisdom, saves, and spells. Those papers were lives. They unfurled scrolls and spoke words to animate the dead. They were cursed by intelligent swords that hungered for the blood of elves. They courted pegasi in old tongues, then soared over hills that billowed green, glacial mountains dusted white, bogs sagging with plague and dead hope. They were honored in Kara-Tur, Greyhawk, and Krynn.

What did I know of white kids gone demonic, Patricia Pulling, and steam tunnels? Fuck the dumb dichotomies and what people think this means. Even then, I was dreaming of Raistlin's black robes one moment, and Dorsett's spin move the next. This was what my father deeded—that our Knowledge of Self be more than America, that we understand the brain death that sprawled from the projects to the subdivisions. Consciousness was a beginning, but the imagination that could turn straight 18s into paladins in plate, could make warrens in tunnels from graph paper, could pull armies of gnolls from miniatures—this was the Knowledge that ultimately would find a way out.

My father was black as the universe, but the doctrinaire could get the bozak. He tried his hand at jewel crafting, until the cadmium almost killed him. Behind our crib on Barrington, he kept bees in a hive of movable frames. On weekends, you'd see him and Brother Howard spacewalking in white masks and giant suits. They'd return with trays of honey and wax. Big Bill would chew the wax like tobacco. The raw honey made me sick. Once a drone stung my mother, and Dad joked that these were the origins of young Menelik, born early that next year.

These were the years where I knew six brothers and sisters were a gorgeous gift. Me and Menelik were the only permanent residents of Barrington Road. But then on weekends—or when Patsy, Selah, or Linda just got sick— any combination of kids could appear, and with them another world. My sister Kris brought boxes of dubbed tapes, put me on to New Edition and later Big Daddy Kane. Bill would ball up socks and pillowcases into a makeshift football, and on our knees we'd crash into one another until someone hit the floor.

Our best days were those weekends, when all the kids flowed through on Friday night. They always stuck me with the itchy cover. I was too young to put up a fight. Saturday, Dad would make pancake batter from scratch, then pull a bottle of Alaga syrup from the fridge and set it in a pan of boiling water. He would fire up his old black griddle and I would stand back and watch. Dad loved to take chances—once he tossed in a can of corn. Another time it was cottage cheese for milk. Either way we all would pile into the kitchen and eat pancakes in stacks of three. When I'd go back for more Dad would claim my stomach was smaller than my eyes.

By noon we were out on the front lawn. Dad would fiddle with his secondhand camera, which hung from a long black strap around his neck. Everyone feared that strap, because Dad could also deploy it to enlighten children and bring them into balance. Ma would arrange us into a giggling pyramid, with Menelik up top. Dad would flick away until Kelly, John, or Kris—someone at the bottom—got restless and shook the core. We'd tumble to the grass like clowns out of a rainbow-colored car, then shove, stumble, and laugh. Ma would step back and pull Menelik close. Dad just flicked away, until these moments were encased in amber.

By Sunday night, it was me and Menelik again, all alone as we were, and I was lost in the sprawl of this house and its many doors, stairs. On Monday, I'd eat a bowl of Chex, grab my lunch, and head up Ayrdale. I'd stop off at Butch's and reveal four nickels, enough for ten Squirrel Nuts and ten lemon cookies. At Callaway Elementary, I'd stand out front, hoping to get a look at big-eyed Terry or her mom. Grandma lived a few blocks away, right off Penhurst. In the daytime she drove a big white car to somewhere near Reisterstown and took care of grown white people who could barely spell their names. Sometimes I'd show up after school, and I will always remember her smiling and saying—Boy, you ain't worth two cents—before making me a plate of french fries.

All my classmates were gifted and talented. But twice a day, Ms. Rhone pulled five or six and took us to a room with a fountain, brown tables, and walls painted sea blue. We tended a hermit crab and came to understand that all animals, even us, have a habitat. All our homework was weird and open-ended. We made dioramas that moved and told stories, and concocted creatures of papier-mâché.

We fielded a team for the Olympics of the Mind. When we practiced, Ms. Rhone played *Danse Macabre*, and the strings jabbed like many shards of ice. Then she'd ask us to meditate on the color blue, and go around the room awarding points to whoever's answers were most surreal. We competed over at the local liberal university and lost to a group of white kids, who looked like they did this thing in their sleep. I fantasized about taking them on again, but that would not happen. At the end of the year my parents removed me from these special classes, because I was screwing up in the part of school that mattered. From that point forward no part of any school mattered to me again.

Dad pushed me out of the island in the sky, citing a sack of problems that I couldn't understand. The oil went too fast. The basement constantly flooded. Mr. Wilder built his fence onto our backyard.

My folks sold the house, and after a stint renting in Edmondson Village, we came to Tioga. This was 1984. I was older. I played Little League football. I traded *World* and *Ranger Rick* for *Computer Gazette*. From the back I'd transcribe programs in BASIC that predicted elections and sent hot air balloons in varying colors falling across the screen. I was like that for a year or so before things changed.

Back in West Baltimore—the landscape gutted, dead eyes all around, and hundreds of kids slain every year from gunshots and bricks to the skull and every other undignified means to their end—it became clear that we were all in proximity to great heaving change. Bill and I couldn't name it, but felt it as a fear that jangled like the change in our pockets when we walked to the corner store. Dad responded to the radicalism of the moment with more radicalism that extended the bounds of rational thought. He refused to buy air-conditioning and insisted Baltimore's muggy summers were best left to Zen: Son, son. The only heat is inside your head.

He deployed many fans, with white plastic cages that swiveled on axes and dual blade systems that could reverse and forward all at once. But all they did was blow the hot air more efficiently. He pushed Black Classic on me even more. He saw me as a special candidate for this. His political harangues had not yet sunk in; still, no one in the house devoured books like me. I read about everything I could find—dolphins and killer whales, volcanoes and alien life, histories of robotics, the gods of ancient Rome. I read to re-treat into other worlds, but these Conscious books Dad pushed were just confirmation of the nightmare. And so the Knowledge of Self piled up next to my bed, unfinished.

No matter. Dad had other ways of making his point. I was impressed into the most mundane and monotonous services. In the garage behind our house Dad kept boxes of Black Classic books. My job was to open each box and place a mailing list card into each book—the idea being that each of these cards would float back from around the world requesting our catalog, and the senders would eventually buy books. On weekends, I might watch wrestling all morning, content in my own frantic idleness. But Dad would have been working since seven, and at noon he would appear and send me out back. I dreamed of a day when I made a dent in the inventory and there would be no more books to card. Instead, every weekend the boxes re-generated and overflowed. For this service I was paid the Paul Coates wage—a dollar an hour and no plucks upside the head. Once I protested—

Me: But this isn't even minimum wage.

Dad: Son, this business puts food on your table. Your minimum wage is the shirt on your back.

This was not true. The press was not profitable. It took food off our table—whatever was left after the basics was reinvested. But in a broader, cosmic sense, he was correct. Black Classic Press—like Lemmel, like the many books suggestively strewn across the house, like Upward Bound— was another tool Dad enlisted to make us into the living manifestations of all that he believed and get us through.

But then, in bed at night, I conspired on many ways out. I thought of allegations of child abuse—certainly this work camp qualified. I thought of matches dropped in the garage, book burning as liberation. I thought about the romance of runaways and living in bus stations with friendly drunks, freight trains that cast about America, and fantasies of squatting in shopping malls where the mannequins came to life when the doors closed. But I never advanced these plans beyond the fantastical mind space that kids reserve for windfall fortunes and birthdays every day. Meanwhile, I was oppressed, persecuted under the rule of this enlightened despot.

The true resistance was led by Big Bill, my bridge to all the illicit and dangerous things that a young man must come to know. Once I came home from a half day at school and found Dante, Jay, and Bill assembled at the table in our small living room, presiding over several bottles. The bottles were filled with different colored liquid, to varying capacity.

Me: Yo, whattup?

Them: (*Glass-eyed nothingness, blank stare, incomprehensible slurring.*)

Me: (*Creeping past to the kitchen.*) Oookkkkaay . . .

Them: (*Looking up, laughing*) Mad dog, mad dog, mad dog!, MAD DOG!

Bill stood up and filled a plastic cup halfway, then passed it to me. Anything to be worthy of manhood and dap. I snatched the cup and took it to the head. It was like Kool-Aid laced with hot sauce. Applause all around.

But more potent than minor acts of rebellion was the new slang Bill brought to bear on our oppressed situation. This was before Eazy-E brunched with Bush, and in radio there was still money to be had in boasting, "No rap." Up North, the new sound was the regional anthem and broadcast to whole communities. But where I was from, the word didn't come around on radio until all the streetlights were lit.

Some of you were there at the proper moment: sprawled across a homeboy's bed, your back to the mattress, tossing a tennis ball to yourself, debating this year's O's. Driving your mother's blue Cressida down Dolfield, and to all your niggers pointing out the window at Charmaine and then "lying" on your dick. In your cousin's basement, clutching a joystick, wondering how they could call this single-player fraud Double Dragon. Then the magic moment, when a homey puts the tape in the deck and everything inside gets very quiet.

In Baltimore the feeling was cultish, and taken in only by a few. The music of the city was the erotic throb of house. I followed Bill, but—even at that young age—believed that the times demanded something that spoke to our chaotic, disfigured, and gorgeous world. Bill's hands were Promethean. He would walk into our small bedroom, toss off his Alabama Starter jacket, throw a tape in the deck, and pump up the volume. Then he'd nod his head to the beat, rhyming along, pointing and waving his hands for emphasis on favorite lines and quips. This was the first music I'd ever known. I'd heard Luther and Deniece Williams, and like all my brethren, I hummed along. But it was nothing that I could own. What I loved about the New York noise was that, like our lives, none of it made sense. Viola loops got the best of me, garbled voice samples flying in from impossible angles, and then where there should have been a bridge, melody, a jangling hook, there were only drums—kicking, booming, angry 808 drums.

Here I am, standing before my small black stereo. Jungle Brothers is spinning on the turntable. Q-Tip pierces the fog with a nativist sword. I am on my third listen and still I do not understand.

They fought back with civil rights
That scarred the soul, it took the sight.

The album is a jumble. I can't tell you what Mike G is running from. I have never heard of the Violators. I scrounge around the house in search of my father's atlas, flip pages until I arrive at a map of their great and mythical realm, Strong Island. I expect a kingdom, but all I see is a bunch of dumb islands waiting to float away.

The mystery, those great expansive plains of unsaid, sucked all of us in. No one knew how Kane came to spit in such a way that the roughest breakbeat turned coquettish, a lady in roses on a Saturday evening stroll. I'd search the liner notes for clues, play back lyrics until they were memory, and then play back memory until I gleaned messages, imagined and real. And slowly I began to pull something from the literature. Slowly I came to understand why these boys needed to wear capes, masks, and muscle suits between bars. Slowly I came to feel that I was not the only one who was afraid.

≡

CHAPTER 4

To teach those
who can't say my name

Big Bill's next step was natural in that age. Across the country black boys were begging their parents for a set of Tech-
nic 1200s and an MPC. Failing that, they banged on lunch
tables and beat boxed until they could rock the *Sanford and
Son* theme song and play it underwater. Up on Wabash, Bill
stood in Marlon's basement, holding the mic like a lover.
They called themselves the West Side Kings, which meant
Marlon cutting breakbeats and Bill reciting battle rhymes

he'd scrawled on a yellow notepad. He would return to Tioga with demos, play them for hours, and rap along with himself. This went on for two years before I saw the West Side Kings in action. By then the game had changed, and brothers had gotten righteous.

That was the summer of 1988—the first great season of my generation. The Grand Incredible was dead, KRS converted to Consciousness and assumed the sentinel pose of Malik Shabazz. All the world's boom boxes were transformed into pulpits for Public Enemy. Before now, the music was escapist and fun—some beats and the dozens, fat chains and gilded belt buckles. But Chuck D pulled us back into the real. He premiered in the colors of Al Davis, did not dance; and when he grabbed the mic, it transformed into the lost rifle of Robert Charles.

Here in Baltimore, brothers would put on the Enemy and recoil. We had never heard anything so grating—drums crashed into whistles, sirens blared off beat. But the cacophony was addictive and everywhere. In the alley behind Liberty, "Don't Believe the Hype" was the loop. On weekends, amid modules, the *Player's Handbook*, and dice, Malik would play "Cold Lamping" and quote Flavor Flav. Dad heard "She Watch Channel Zero?!" and pointed at Ma—That's how I feel about them damn romance novels.

She reads. She reads. She reads. I was a reluctant convert but captured by the many layers, the hints at revelation, and a sound that I did not so much enjoy as I felt compelled to understand. Every track was a disheveled history of music. And armed with an array of sonics, Chuck D came forward and revealed a new level of Knowledge.

His style was baffling. I caught disjointed phrases and images, times and places that did not cohere—"goddamn Grammys," a "government of suckers," "they see me, fear me." By the tenth session, the sonic blur sharpened into a recovered collective memory. The story began in our glory years with the banishing of Bull Conner and all his backward dragons. Never had the mountaintop seemed so close at hand. But marching from victory we stumbled into a void. And now we were here in the pit, clawing out one another's eyes. We were all—even me—so angry. We could not comprehend how it came to this. Dad tried to explain the Fall, but he was an elder and full with his own agenda. Chuck was one of us, and once we got it, we understood that he spoke beautifully in the lingua franca of our time. He took us back to '66, showed us Hoover and his array of phone taps, the grafted devils with their drugs and guns like pox blankets for Indians. We fell, blinded, corrupted, consumed by Reaganomics, base heads, and black on black. But now was the hour of '88. Now was the time to reverse our debased years, to take over, grab our guns again, and be men.

By then I had met the great lion, Afeni Shakur, most famous of the Panther 21. She'd moved to Baltimore some years earlier, and among the Conscious she was legend. Afeni was an old comrade of my father's, but when the Panthers went to war with one another, they came down on different sides. They had comrades who'd killed their comrades, but, still in all, through another decade, the human touch pulled them back together.

I had heard the tales, and measured against the everyday sameness of my father, Afeni was large. But the legend was human—she smiled when she saw me, cooked spaghetti, and found my baby brother amusing. Her son and daughter spent time among us. Bill and Tupac traded lyrics. I took Sekyiwa to see *Snow White*. But even then their clan was glamorous and of that final faction that held out a Marxist hope of the empire's ruin.

Here is how it all came together: Bill, Sekyiwa, all of us, we knew who we were, in the rote manner of knowing where two streets intersect. But anything more than that, a feeling for why any kid would grab a black beret, guns, and law books was only partially there. I was slowly coming to a dawning, and then one afternoon Sekyiwa and me sat on my bedroom floor pumping "Rebel Without a Pause"— "Hard—my calling card / Recorded and ordered—supporter of Chesimard."

Sekyiwa looked up. That's my aunt. Rather her aunt's slave name. But Sekyiwa only partially understood how the name Chesimard had come to Chuck D.

The next day I went to my father for the story. The story was all of two sentences, and then Dad reaching up to his bookshelf for the Knowledge of Self. On the cover, her face was off center. She wore an Afro and glanced over her shoulder. On the cover was her name—Assata Shakur. I'd started down this path a few months earlier, burrowing through *African Glory,* a book my father republished. But now I truly became a seeker. This was not my father's story and then it was; for there, inside the tale of one Panther, was the story of them all. The cowboy impulse took me first—the thought that I, for all my awkward hands and Krazy-Glued glasses, was rebel blood; and that thought filled me with a stupid, childish pride. But all of us need myths. And here out West, where we all had lost religion, had taken to barbarian law, what would be our magic? What would be sacred words?

I took to Consciousness because there was nothing else, no other sorcery to counter death for suede, leather, and gold. My father bet his life on change. For the glory of ex-cons, abandoned mothers, and black boys lost, he had made peace with his end. I was a coward, mostly concerned with getting from one day to the next. How could I square my young life with this lineage? What would I say to the theology of my father, which held that the Conscious Act was worth more than sex, bread, or even drawn breath?

There were no answers in the broader body, where the best of us went out like Sammy Davis and spoke like there had never been war. I will avoid the cartoons—the hard rocks loved Billy Ocean, Luther was classic, and, indeed, I did sit in my seventh period music class eyeing Arletta Holly and humming "Lost in Emotion." But you must remember the era. Niggers were on MTV in lipstick and curls, extolling their exotic quadroons, big-upping Fred Astaire, and speaking like the rest of us didn't exist. I'm talking S-curls and sequins, Lionel Richie dancing on the ceiling. I'm talking the corporate pop of Whitney, and Richard Pryor turning into the toy. Was like Parliament had never happened, like James Brown had never hit. All our champions were disconnected and dishonored, handing out Image Awards, while we bled in the streets.

But now the word turned Conscious, De La refused to scowl and Stetsasonic shouted across the Atlantic gap. First, Chuck, then KRS, and then everywhere you looked MCs were reaching for Garvey's tricolor, shouting across the land, self-destruction was at an end, that the logic of white people's ice had failed us, that the day of awareness was now.

Across the land, the masses fell sway to the gospel. Old Panthers came out in camouflage to salute Chuck D. Cold killers would get a taste of "Raise the Flag," drop their guns, and turn vegan. Brothers quoted Farrakhan with wine on their breath. Harlots performed *salaat*, covered their blond french rolls in mud cloth and royal kente. Dark girls slashed their Apollonia posters, burned their green contacts, cut their hair, threw in braids. Gold was stashed in the top dresser drawer. The fashion became your father's dashiki, beads, and Africa medallions.

The music boosted the words of my father, though he only partially understood. He was frustrated by me, even as my Consciousness bloomed. He kept a notebook chronicling my slow progress: *Ta-Nehisi came to work ten minutes late today. He then spent fifteen minutes in the bathroom. He worked for ten minutes. He then spent fifteen more minutes in the bathroom. He came out and played with Menelik.* He was trying to shape us before the winter age of eighteen, and change, though coming, was never fast enough.

But we were changing. Big Bill was touched by the transformation, trading the everyday struggle for the Struggle. The same music that pulled me out of my fog, left him reeling. Again and again he went back to the lab, reveled in mourning bass lines, and crafted sweeping images of the great Satan's fall. They added Joey on the keyboard, changed the group's name to the Foundation, and switched their sound until it was holy and urging rebellion. I played his tapes along with all the others, and began to understand.

I was twelve, but when I heard "Lyrics of Fury"—"A horn if you want the style I possess / I bless the child, the earth, the gods, and bomb the rest"—I put away childish things, went to the notebook, and caged myself between the blue lines. In the evenings, that summer, I would close the door, lay across the bed, and put pen to pad.

At first I felt the words of others pulsing through me—my reforming brother, the esoteric allusions of The God, the philosophy of KRS-One—and in truth, in many years of trying, I never completely touched my own. My hand was awkward; and when I rhymed, the couplets would not adhere, punch lines crashed into bars, metaphors were extended until they derailed off beat. I was unfit, but still I had at it for days, months, and ultimately years. And the more ink I dribbled onto the page, the more I felt the blessing of the Jedi order of MCs. I wrote every day that summer, rhymed over B-side instrumentals, until my pen was a Staff of the Dreaded Streets (plus five chance to banish fools on sight) and my flow, though flicted and disjointed, a Horn of Ghetto Blasting. The words were all braggadocios, but when done with the recital, even though I was alone, I felt bigger.

I'd walk outside, and my head was just a little higher, because if you do this right, if you claim to be that nigger enough, though you battle only your bedroom mirror, there is a part of you that believes. That was how I came to understand, how I came to know why all these brothers wrote and talked so big. Even the Knowledged feared the streets. But the rhyme pad was a spell book—it summoned asphalt elementals, elder gods, and weeping ancestors, all of whom had your back. That summer, I knew what Fruitie was trying to say, that when under the aegis of hip-hop, you never lived alone, you never walked alone.

I harried Big Bill until he took me up to Wabash to spit a sloppy verse. Marlon had cordoned off his father's basement. He presided over the 1200s, spinning breakbeats. Joey played with the keys until he found a riff he liked. I just sat on the couch going over my rhymes, while Bill stood blessing the mic behind what was once a bar.

By then I had raided the tall box of my father's old collection of Black Panther newspapers, devoured them during off-hours in Dad's office, and scribbled allusions to them in my book of rhymes. Dad no longer had to assign readings. My comics collections lapsed. Cartoons felt nonessential. I plunged into my father's books of Consciousness that he'd shelved in nearly every room in the house. That was how I found myself, how I learned my name. All my life Dad had told me what I was, that Ta-Nehisi was a nation, the ancient Egyptian name for the mighty Nubians to the south, but I could not truly hear. Where I'm from,

Tamika is an American name. But Ta-Nehisi was hyphened and easily bent to the whims of anyone who knew the rudiments of the dozens. But seeing that handle among the books of glorious Africa, I knew why I could never be Javonne or Pete, that my name was a nation, not a target, not something for teachers to trip over but the ancient Nubians and the glorious Egyptians of the 25th.

I felt a light flowing through me. I awoke, excited, hungry to understand this immediate world, how we had all fallen to this. Now I knew Lemmel in a fuller sense, that it was troubled because all things worth anything ultimately are. That my world, though mired in disgrace, was more honorable than anything, was more beautiful than the exotic counties way up Reisterstown and Liberty Road. All the Mondawmins of the world—with their merchant vultures, wig stores, sidewalk sales, sub shops, fake gold, bastard boys, and wandering girls—were my only home. That was Knowledge and Consciousness joined, and when I grabbed the mic, that was the alchemy I brought forth. When I was done, I emerged taller, my voice was deeper, my arms were bigger, ancestors walked with me, and there in my hands, behold, Shango's glowing ax.

Big Bill was gone much more now. He'd done a little better in school, and Dad rewarded him with leave time at his mother's. No more veggie sausage. No more books. No more yard work. He yelled, I'm out of here! as he walked out the door. More frequently I found myself alone. Menelik was four and not allowed to play beyond our brick front porch. My brothers Malik and John were entering their last years of high school. So I went out on my own, and in search of whatever else I did not know, pedaled my double-gooseneck dirt bike up Burlief to the alley and observed.

The boys would be picking up for three on three, and I was always picked last or not picked at all. On the short granite wall, off to the side, I'd sit next to the boom box, rapping and pantomiming along. I had spent so much time in my room that by now I had the lyrics, pacing, and breath control down. I could untangle the meaning and many syllables of "The Symphony" or deliver the sick monotone of "I'm Housing." This came to be known, among the boys my age, as a talent and they would gather around and request various renditions. Then we'd spend the next few hours debating Kane versus The God.

And then there was basketball, my people's national pastime. I was more enthralled by the violent grace of Steve Atwater and Ronnie Lott. I'd joined the cult of Len Bias, but after he fell—dead from a coke-induced heart attack at twenty-three—I left the rock alone. But Magic and Kareem were still paragons in the alley. Niggers would throw the blind pass or sky hook and call out their names like a spell that could conjure the proper spin on the ball.

There was no magic for me. I couldn't take two dribbles without a carry or walk. My jumper careened over backboards. My foul shots were all left of the rim. That was a cause for much laughter and jokes. But so was something about everyone, in everything else. Most of us had something wrong, and all it took was the right Larry Young, David Pridgett, or Big Bill to call out your girl feet, enlarged nose, busted shape up and summarily cut you to pieces. What I came to understand was the great democracy in this, and that what mattered to these boys was not so much what you came to the street with but how you carried what you were given.

So I took control. I stopped letting Dad cut my hair and instead took seven bones to the barbershop over at Mondawmin, avoiding old men and women, and came back with a tight fade. I stood out in the alley, called next, chose up, snatched boards and kicked it back out, put a hand up, and moved with my man. I talked less and watched more. I assessed the mood of every area I walked through, then altered my bearing to the action which seemed most likely to unfold. I got down with the local clique. Leroy, who saved me from the Hilton-Beys, was the nominal head. There was Bo, who lived further up Liberty, close to Community College of Baltimore. Brock and Dante, the lucky ones, whose parents sent them off to private school. There were two other half brothers, whose names I will not mention, because we thought their mother was on crack. They lived in a large, crumbling house. Rats creeped out the back. Mostly they all were the products of single parents, and in the most tragic category—black boys, with no particular criminal inclinations but whose very lack of direction put them in the crosshairs of the world.

But from them I acquired large portions of the Knowledge. We set out into Baltimore. We'd catch the bus up to Reisterstown for the movies, and bust out the No Home Training, laughing and talking louder than normal, in that stupid teenage manner. We'd catch the subway downtown to yell rude things at honeys near the harbor. I became secure in the numbers, and noticed that if I walked like the boys around me, smiled only when essential, it all became a little easier. Over at Mondawmin, soldiers caught solo would see our numbers, and though we were still a nameless crew without a rep, they turned and headed the other way. Still, I was a stepchild here. I never pulled tool and went Larry Davis. I had no ill visions of Nino Brown. But now I knew that this was not chaos, that the streets were a country and like all others, the streets had anthems, culture, and law. I was not bred a patriot. But that summer I became a soldier. In September, I stepped off the porch with a new swing and bop. Lemmel, fed up with brawls and stickup kids, mandated uniforms and transparent knapsacks. I bought a blue net bag, which was a statement of cool among us, placed a thin canvas binder inside, then slung it over my shoulder. The declaration of uniforms made all gear equal, except for kicks. I turned to my mother, who was never adverse to the style of the day, and emerged in Travel Fox and Rockports.

Plus I was not alone. We would start off only five or six deep, trooping down Tioga, down Gwynns Falls, and then up the grass hill. But all of us had boys from other districts, and as we traveled you would see a homeboy from summer camp or elementary, whose clique would be assimilated, and in this way we would expand until, atop Dukeland hill, dap was exchanged, and we were many deep. We'd front at the top of the concrete steps, talking shit, cultivating rage until we were ice grilled, until our movements were warning flares and bared teeth.

Then I was alone again, because initially none of my crew was gifted and talented. I soloed into the next level of the Marshall Team—8-16, fewer boys this time, and that meant trouble. Our army was smaller now and could not tolerate pacifists. I remembered who I'd been just a year earlier, spaced out and ready to run, and wanted no part of it. I thought of walking in, smacking the first fool I saw, and taking a suspension like a badge. But that was just the voice of my intelligent armor. I was still a dreamer, if now repressed, was still cupcakes and comic books at the core.

My teachers were more intense, because this was the first big year of our lives, the year that decided which high school we'd get into. In English class, we sat in rows five deep. My counselor Mr. Webster—white, bespectacled, and kind—handed out booklets filled with all our possibilities. Inside were the descriptions of all of Baltimore's magnet schools, their profiles, requirements, and varying spheres of specialty, running the gamut from music to English to ROTC to engineering and math. I was, still am, a scientist at heart, and aimed for Baltimore Polytech, best school in the city and home to all our future Garrett Morgans and Charles Drews. But there were bigger reasons—in all things, our first concern was security and what we saw in the citywide schools was not great academics but cessation of gun law, a place of reprieve if only because everyone there had come by choice. The classroom came second.

In the new year we shared our gym period with our inverse, 8-07. They walked in with a mean slouch and sat on the other side of the gym bleachers. There was not one girl among them—they were thirty deep, bigger, seemed that they had failed many grades many times. I just sat back silent, Nobody Smiling, told myself I was not afraid. We shared lockers and so as soon as I saw them, I knew 8-07 would try to test us in the locker room. My buddy Jermaine pulled me off to the side and gave me the briefing—Tana, you better not go out like no punk.

I was one of the tallest boys in my class by now, and had acquired enough Knowledge to know that 8-07 would step to me first. My height made me the symbolic head of our squad, even if I had sought no such title. After class, while I got dressed in the locker room, I was awaiting one of the big kids, one of the ones who seemed that he should be off enlisting or driving a truck. Instead, they sent a bizarro, a tall awkward freak with thick glasses and an unfortunate head. He was not a natural, and loped around the locker room like he'd spent the previous year dusting off his jeans and taping his glasses. I understood his bearing, how feeling like you'd do anything to avoid a repeat makes you snarl a little quicker than what, even by the standards of the streets, is reasonable.

But this kid had gotten it worse.

They gathered and he advanced my way. I'd been preparing for this all summer. In my mind I heard the 808 kick and did not speak but raised my dukes. This was my first scrap, the first time I'd felt anger as lighter fluid. This kid was disrespect, an attempt to show that the weakest among them could dominate the biggest among us. And, too, there was the fact that in his weakness I saw a self that I wanted to erase. I swung.

What followed was not glorious and triumphant but a blind rolling around, many badly aimed blows striking steel lockers. It ended in mutual choke holds. Our camps pulled us apart. 8-07 grabbed their net bags and filed out before us.

It wasn't long before Big Bill was duly deposited back to Tioga. That was the pattern of things. He would steady his ship for a while, earn a reprieve, then return to his earlier self and be condemned to Dad's care. Linda, Dad, and Ma were all trying to drag him toward the promised land. He was still caught in between, juggling the new Consciousness with everything the streets had told him since he first stood on a corner. Either way, he was about the girls, the mic, and the need to be loved by immediate people, places, and things.

Love was how he got caught up. All boys were judged by arm strength, our varying ability to turn chance encounters into digits and then belt notches. Bill was tall, stylish, and kept a fresh fade. But most important, he did not half step, mumble, or stare at the ground. That certitude was in demand among the girls we knew, in fact, was a prerequisite to any exchange. And so Bill became profligate with the jennys and then, later, sloppy. The girl showed up at Linda's house in need of some recognition, a sliver of respect. Bill answered the door. He did not usher her in. Linda sat in the back.

She had come up pregnant weeks earlier. Bill had agreed to cover half, and she'd agreed to not bring in any adults. But the child in my brother still caged him. Half of him hoped the whole deal would just vanish. The other half was just dead wrong. Bill played her to the left, did not answer her calls, and went off in pursuit of other pleasures. All she wanted was for him to honor his word. They argued. She yelled and banged on the door. He ordered her to adjust her tone. She didn't and now he became angry, grabbed all, maybe, hundred pounds of her, and slammed her to the ground.

That was enough to bring out Linda—

Have you lost your mind? I didn't raise you to put your hands on women. Get in the damn house.

Inside, old girl broke it down, while Bill sat and stewed. Of course it was out of his hands now. Linda called Dad and Bill was ordered to be responsible for his half and make the trek out Route 40 to a country clinic and see the thing done.

After that, Dad cut Bill loose. They'd been at war all his life, but now Bill was seventeen, a grown man in my father's eyes, and mostly set on whatever path would be. He was remanded back to Tioga, but there was no more checking homework, reviewing report cards, or upbraidings for cutting class. Dad issued the simple ultimatum that all of

us lived under—at eighteen you will leave this house—
and left the rest in the hands of Big Bill.

Back at Lemmel, the Marshall Team came to an understanding with 8-07. A few fights followed mine, but
once respect was assured, our meetings lost their sinister
edge and diffused into the everyday roughhousing of boys
anywhere. In our second semester, we took gym alone and
were left to spar with one another. The boys were still desperate to prove their hand speed and ability to dominate.
Me, I just threw enough combos to send the message that I
was willing, a few slaps to keep the peace. That accom-
plished, I came to an accord with my gifted brothers.

There were only seven or eight of us, but a year earlier they could not help but broadcast their contempt whenever I was near. Now, we would build on what we had in
common: an obsession with Dan Marino's rifle. At lunch,
we would spread the lore of Mike Tyson, how he knocked
niggers out southpaw, how they danced as they fell, rose,
and fell again. Our deepest dream was to move through the
world with that sort of constant thundering force. Failing
that, we banded together and tried to project an aura that
guarded against assault.

My pre-school ritual came to include a larger circle of
friends. The gifted kids had to be bused in from deeper sec-

tions of the West Side. They altered their trajectory and would stop and meet on my porch in the morning. Then we would begin our march forward, shielded by the security of one another. I swooned in the turnaround, and marveled at my own power to remake myself not at some private or county school, where I was unknown, but here on my own soil where once I'd feared for my skin.

On weekends, I did projects for school and wrote rhymes. I played tapes of Gil Scott, Malcolm's "Message to the Grass Roots," and continued my quest to ingest anything in my father's book collection relating to the Panthers. It was all so romantic to me. I'd replaced one pantheon for another, Spider-Man and Goose for Robert Williams and Huey. This was not joyful, exactly, but offered me freedom. I could not escape who I was, but now didn't want to. My new heroes and narrative gave meaning to everything I'd once hated about my life—the banned holidays and fasts, the assigned reading, the angry young boys all around me. Dad noticed, but uttered not a word of pride. Still, I knew how he got down, reserved, with most of his more positive emotions inferred.

I carved out safety at Lemmel, but knew that if I could go to a school where I did not require a security detail, I should do it. My sights were set on the majestic stature of Baltimore Polytech and its twin school Western. In my early days down near Mondawmin, Kris was a junior at Western. On school days we would take the same train to West Cold Spring. I would walk a few blocks over to fifth grade. Kris would wait on the street under the elevated subway tracks. Often I'd see her bus, the number 33 with Poly/Western scrolling electronically across the front, and I thought it incredible that two schools could hold such sway that mass transit was turned to charter.

The Poly/Western complex was a royal seat in Baltimore. Once they were the exclusive domain of white kids in uniforms. Now like all the old white neighborhoods with prewar homes and yawning streets, they were ours. But unlike everything else we inherited, the great traditions carried on. Western was the oldest all-girl public school in the country. It emerged as a funnel to exclusive schools in the Northeast. Traditions were minted. Big sister juniors adopted little sister freshmen. Seniors wore all white to inaugurate the start of the year. The mascot was the dove. The basketball team was hot and dominant.

Poly stood across the quad, equally venerable and exclusive. Once all boys, it had gone progressive, admitted girls, integrated before any other high school in the city. No boys of sense disputed the presence of young women. Besides, the old ways endured—the orange and blue colors, the great football teams, the rivalry with City College, and most important a steady stream of young scientific minds. Everyone from Poly/Western went to college.

I did well that year, which for me meant a high C, and only one beating from Dad or Ma. I must have done really well, because I don't even remember who administered it. I was always better when the repercussions were immediate, and the threat of heading to my zoned high school sent me to homework and study. They notified us in the spring. It was like a miniature ritual of college admissions. You could tell that we were different in the gifted program, because while most of the school knew where they were headed, we buzzed with expectation. No one wanted to go to their zoned school.

When I got the news, my mother was at home. I do not remember the color of the envelope or the length of the letter. But I remember jumping up and down and hugging my mother. I remember her smiling at me in actual pride, and this was new. She was often proud of me and demonstrated as much, but it was over potential and possibility, something I had said which made her expect that at some unknowable future date, I would amount to something more than what I seemed to be. Now she smiled at the tangible, at the real, not at what I dreamed I'd be but at that moment what I *was*.

It was the season of expectations for all of us. Dad had left Bill to his fate. Bill, though oriented to the streets, still had enough wits to know that no one ever pulled a girl by bragging about being a high school dropout. Bill did not even bother applying anywhere aside from the Mecca. By now he'd visited Kris and Kell, had seen the parties, which were next level, and had some sense that college was more than a collection of eyeglasses. That was enough to pull from him the first mature effort of his life—and thus the first meaningful result. He was accepted, the third among three that Dad had steered to Howard.

The rest of my year felt easy and musical. Classes were more relaxed. I wrote rhymes at night. All of us were anticipating the annual eighth-grade trip to Patapsco State Park. My mother took me shopping up at Reisterstown. I bought a fresh blue sweat suit with a matching Duke tee shirt, Starter hat, and a pair of blue-and-white Airs. Afterward we ate fried chicken, corn, greens, and biscuits. I dressed the next day with pride—I had never been so in style in all my life. We were told to bring our boom boxes and dress in our flyest gear. Teachers provided food for a cookout, footballs and softball equipment. They piled us into buses and rolled us out of the dense city for a forty-minute drive into the open. I rolled down the cheese bus window and tasted the air. I had hayfever then, but it must not have mattered because I don't remember a single sneeze or eye rub.

We walked all across the state park that day, tossing the football, running routes and calling out *Henry Ellard* or *Jerry Rice*. And that's when we saw them coming over the hill, running our way. We were not the only middle-school seniors on the trip. 8-07 in all their deep glory were running down an asphalt path. We made them from a distance, and, not knowing what to expect, we were ready and we were cocked.

We did not run, and as they closed, it became clear that we could never escape, the mentality of war must always be at the ready. Someone would have had a boom box. I like to think "Brothers Gonna Work It Out" was on the deck. But that would be a year too soon. This was spring 1989. I was still a reluctant warrior, artless and gauche. But I had done the Knowledge, and pledged my unwieldy ax to upholding the code.

They slowed down as they came to us, out of breath, some of them putting hands on their knees. They began laughing and a few of us started to soften our stance. But I stood off to the side, confused and convinced that whatever respect was accorded to the other brothers could never extend to me. One of them approached me—What's up, nigger?—and extended his arm. I tightened in a mix of fear and frustration. I thought of how this would end, just as it began. But then he smiled. I looked down and saw his open hand, universal and at peace. I reached out and gave him a pound.

CHAPTER 5

This is the Daisy Age

I wore a powder-blue short-sleeved shirt, matching navy Travel Fox, and stonewashed jeans. I had a green tie-dye book bag, with twin yellow ropes in place of straps. The back festooned with buttons, the totems of my champions—Bob Marley, Marcus Garvey, Malcolm X. Nigger, I was fly—my cut, two days old, tops. The angles of my lineup could have (the chains, freed the slaves. Likely, I hung a wooden ankh from my neck. Likely, I was armed with Knowledge of Self—*The COINTELPRO Papers* or *A Panther Is a Black Cat.*

I was thirteen, but I carried that thing, stepped off the porch with the bop of God's son, floated across the black parking lot of Mondawmin, paid my fare, descended the cavernous escalators, then trained up to Rogers station. I was still a transfer and bus ride away, and yet I was overcome by status. Through all my terror and trembling, through all my torpor and dim wits, I had conjured this passport into the royal city. I wish I had paused on that long subway platform, closed my eyes, and inhaled. I wish I had acknowledged the feeling, held it close, and understood that it was not forever. But I was young and immortal, so I bounded down two escalators, walked a few yards, then emerged into the sunny basin beneath the station.

Word to Mark Garvey, the West Side was in effect. Everyone had run through Charley Rudo's, High Energy, Shoe City, and Robert C's, until we emerged with piles and piles of school clothes that would have us styling for months. Rogers Avenue was humming, dozens of buses bound for everywhere pulled in and out of their hubs. Kids gathered in smiling packs, more free than any school children I'd seen in two years. I was alone, but now Original Man and unafraid. I had survived jumpings and kids in hoodies, hands in deep pockets threatening to pull out. I had survived my father, his many books and hands that were boulders. I had survived the shadow of Big Bill and emerged not a man of streets but of Knowledge.

I stood off to the side, all Nobody Smiling, affecting a measure of cool, representing William H. Lemmel. I caught the publicly chartered 33. Poly/Western scrolled across the front like destiny. When I boarded at Rogers it was half full, but as we rolled down Wabash and across Cold Spring Lane it swelled with other kids like me but not. They were gifted, but had been sheltered in more forgiving schools and hailed from neighborhoods with detached houses and lawns built for tackle football in the fall. This was still the West Side, and so they wore the reserve of that shackled land. But they had reclaimed their laughter, and deployed it without regard for weakness or what it might say.

I had spent that summer in early college prep out at the nearby campus for the University of Maryland, yet another of the programs my parents were always putting us in, hoping that whatever messages we missed from them might connect from another angle. For a month, I lived in a dorm with kids cropped from all over the city. We bunked together in suites, and during the day took lectures in the sciences and field trips to various points of interest in the city. We ate in the school cafeteria. Our downtime was spent swimming, hanging out in the dorm lobby, watching cable videos, or sitting outside our rooms bumping "Back to

Life" on our boom boxes. Fridays our parents came for us, or we boarded the 20 bus and looked out the windows as it wended its way through the roads and stations of the open county. There were talent shows. A few of us lip-synched Slick Rick's "A Children's Story." I was the narrator. My boy Isaac acted it out, snatched the lady, pulled the automatic.

At night, suite doors were left unlocked and jimmys and jennys would float through each other's rooms. We did not know what to make of the girls or of ourselves, but felt the deepest need to express the burgeoning adult inside. Kiesha breached the portal of my room at a heathen hour. The dawning light from outside woke me up, and against the darkness, she was angelic. During the day our conversations had been friendly and vague. She was slender, brown, and from Cherry Hill, where they beat niggers with scrap metal and threw 'em off the Key Bridge. We had exchanged numbers and had talks on three-way. She lay down next to me with her hands around her chest.

Are you good? I asked.

She said something affirmative. I went back to sleep. The next morning, all the girls giggled and asked if I was gay. They were so advanced. I was only thirteen. This was 1989. There were still things I did not understand.

We dismounted the 33 bus in front of the campus, and joined a gathering throng buzzing about the first day. I was amped, but played low-key. I scouted immediately for girls, and what I saw disrupted cognition. There were honeys from across the city—Westport, Hollander Ridge, Gwynn Oak, Northwood. They were everything from redbone to yo-yo darkskin. The dimes among them carried Benetton bags, were dolled up like Lily Powers—finger waves, a head of dyed blond, and eyes like enchanted daggers. I saw we were outnumbered, as brothers who try the civilized way always are. But in this instance, it was thrilling.

I caught flashbacks, and saw faces that took me back to Callaway Elementary and Ms. Rhone. I saw a few from that summer at UMBC, and two or three from Lemmel. There was no bell that I remember. We just all filed in at the proper time, and made our way to homerooms inscribed on letters we'd received some days before. Here I found my first white teacher, bespectacled, old, and balding, a hold-over from the days when Poly was a different fraternity. We were a different breed, cut from something different than the boys he first taught or the old teachers in short-sleeved white shirts with ties and inconspicuous haircuts.

Poly changed with the culture and demography of Baltimore. It was now our time. The pall was slowly coming off, and we were recovering from crack, though still caught in the aftershocks. I worried less about getting jumped. Weathermen talked more sun. Reports of school shootings were replaced with black is back. Chuck D still preached: Elvis was exposed. Our heroes did not appear on stamps. At night, I pumped "Strictly Snapping Necks" and brought forth lyrics. My daydreams were all on stage. It was black and silent, until I raised my ax and touched the mic with literature and fables.

Big Bill was transitioning into life at the Mecca. In his dorm, among the piles of clothes and kicks, the CDs and tapes, the yellow notebooks of lyrics, he packed his gun. He was charged with the possibilities of this second life—no regulations, no chores, the chance to burn consecutive Els. And he was slowly evolving. He carried a couple of Dad's books and began to feel the call of the People. But he feared the loss of his essence, a slow erosion of the extrasensory gifts imparted by the streets. College was a cartoon to him, flush with bumblers, gophers, and kids who could calculate the temperature on Mars but could not tell you the time. Bill was moved by laws of survival. He was a soldier, insistent that he would not be caught out there. But the "out there" was bigger than he ever dreamed.

His prejudice melted in his first week. He found his eggheads, for sure, walking the city like it couldn't happen, and returning to campus battered, scraped, and a few bills lighter. But this was the Mecca—the incredible cosmopolis of blackness. Nigger, the whole campus was radioactive.

White folks would roll through aimlessly, catch a tan, and start quoting Cabral. There were legacies in their third generation. There were Greeks leaping across the Yard. There were dime pieces, thousands, all different shapes, flavors, and accents. There were kids in cultures and sub-cultures, organizing around robotics, badminton, real estate and Baha'i.

There was the campus, infused with the spirits of alumni, who jettisoned lives and careers for the People's war. The great halls, like at Lemmel, were named for patri-ots—Douglass, Drew, Tubman, and Bethune. There were football games, where in the midst of the school song, the crowd would yell out in time, "It's not a white school!" There were classes, where debates glowed and stretched into the hallways. It could have been anything from Con-tras to global warming, but the filter was always Garvey's. The effect of it all—the ancestral ghosts, the naming rites, the seminars—was a shared consciousness, a constant drumming that promised a new, more advanced Knowl-edge.

Bill was dazzled, and amid all the sects, he found his own—survivors hailing from the ruins of Lansing, New York, Detroit, who'd seized the gift and advanced. Down at Sutton Hall, they convened over blunts—the antidrug of our generation. Cocaine had turned their childhoods spas-tic and sensational. They flew through preteens in speeding cars. All the lovely scenery of puberty and just beyond, first kisses and fucks, were blurred with murder rates and babies breeding babies. Everything happened too fast. So they founded cults of forest fire, then huddled in ciphers and passed. The burning bush was "Kumbaya," a group hug, a chance to slow shit down.

Where others saw the love moment, Bill saw his chance. Their ritual was to put in together for a dime sack. But half the session was spent moaning over headache weed and not enough blunts. Bill was too original for that, thought it would be better to save up some paper, step up his game to an ounce, sell enough for re-up, and keep the profit for his personal. In that fashion he became the dorm connect, and that status plugged him into networks around campus not unlike the ones he'd enjoyed back home. He got bent and partied with his new friends. After class, they dribbled the rock to the local court and, understanding the rules, stayed together to ward off these D.C. niggers who took them for college soft. Bill had his close shaves. At the court, he was always running his mouth, dunking on the underregulation rim, then bellowing and beating his chest. One local soldier got tired of the talk, went to the car, and came back swinging an aluminum bat through air. But Bill was cool. He knew that at any moment, he could reach into his dip and unveil the last word.

The family expanded. I had not been back to Barrington Road in years and, since Lemmel, had ceased all fantasies about a return. The magical house was sold to the Solomons, a young couple with a son a year younger than me. The father was Wellis. The mother was Jovett. The son was Kier. Back when Dad was first selling it, the Solomons would visit us on weekends, handling the sort of real estate arcane, which children have no desire to comprehend. Me and Kier would stand on the front lawn tossing the football, or sword fight with sticks and the tops of metal trash cans. It was to be one of those brief friendships that dot childhood and disappear at the end of parental business.

But then the Solomons returned, trilling the dirge of our time—no father. Dad and Ma sat in Jovett's living room—a misdirected package had brought them there—and the small talk gradually extended and swelled. Wellis had passed away. Jovett was alone, not working, and charged with a son. Dad had turned conservative, but not in the way of the demonologists who sold us out for tenure and crumbs. More like a man who spurns the false talk of revolution for the humbler mission of resurrecting one soul at a time. One of his order had fallen. Who would carry his colors and sword?

My folks went home and talked about their needs. They both commuted to Washington for work and ran the Press by night and weekends. From time to time, they hired folks to man the shop. Business was growing. They'd gone from a few J. A. Rogers pamphlets and a desktop press to becoming a lynchpin of the Baltimore Conscious, their books sold all over the country. They would need more. Jovett came to work in the basement of Tioga, and grew closer and closer to the family. Her son was a brother to me by circumstance. He would come to the house after school and wait for his mother to get off, or on weekends if she happened to be working.

We were not the same—like Bill, the street life made him glow, while I was convinced that there was no future for me out there. But I was mischievous enough and, like most boys, out to test the limitations of the world. Kier was a year younger, but this was not knowable from the way we rolled. We would go up to the alley and shoot on the crate or catch midnight features down at Harbor Park. We paid off winos to buy us forties of Red Bull and, while sauced, tried to walk in a straight line and touch our noses.

Our mothers united on their common charges. Though we were both a couple years away, they started a program of practice SATs. We were drilled on vocabulary and math and taught guessing strategies. My mother had been pushing kids all her adult life. At night, Ma and Jovett would drive down to the Blue Caribbean and salsa with the men. They vacationed in Barbados and then Jovett and Kier joined us on our yearly pilgrimage to my mother's homeland—the Maryland Eastern Shore. We stayed with Aunt Toppie. She made us waffles for breakfast. We were a family beyond borders.

My Consciousness grew, until I was obsessed with having been birthed in the wrong year. All the great wars had been fought, and I was left to rummage through the myths of my fathers. But oh how I longed to take the rope for John Brown or snuff the peon who dimed out Vesey. I would hang out at bookstores built for the people, flipping through Chancellor Williams and Kwame Ture. I put "Ballot or the Bullet" on my Walkman, pinned more buttons of Garvey in imperial regalia to my book bag, and wore a tee shirt with the authoritarian motto "One God. One Aim. One Destiny." I read *The Iceman Inheritance* and flirted with the supremacy of melanin. We had been down so long, and were desperate for anything that told us we were something more. So we embraced the charlatans and their stupid science, until all the old mythologies were remixed and the savages were not drummers and dancers but Hera and Thor.

I became a plague upon my father's books. He treasured them as much for what they said as for what they were. But I cared only for what was inside. I devoured the books, then flung them aside like emptied husks. My father found the ripped-up cover of *Die Nigger Die!* and pushed me to the floor. He did not ban me, instead, after cooling down, explained that I was living in a temple and privy to

Knowledge that many had forgotten. What I owed in return was some reverence and tribute.

But I was a chaotic mind. When obsessed, I wanted only what I wanted and could give no attention to other matters. Urges would whisk through me every fifteen minutes, each one discarding the former. I could not focus. In a white room, sealed and empty, perhaps. But against all the incipient impulses of manhood, I was one big glass jaw. At school, I became a problem, and by the end of my first semester, I was failing three classes. I considered myself capable of student awards and honor, and sometimes I even longed for them. But I longed more to live in my own head, emerging only to laugh or watch the streets on my way home.

I believed in the intellect of all of us, that mine was the legacy that aligned pyraminds and spotted the rings of distant planets with only the naked eye. That was my great inheritance. But I turned this good news to bad ends, and ran with the sort of crew that surveyed all these new teachers, and picked out the ones who would never understand. The ones who should have been out at Bryn Mawr or Calvert Hall. They did not know where we were from. And this was my out. We would sit in the back of the class talking during lectures and throwing paper balls at girls. I asked for bathroom breaks every ten minutes, and then walked the halls making dumb faces at friends in other classes. I prayed for substitutes, would walk in, stare them down like, *you know what this is*, and then it was on—paper footballs flying, the end of assigned seating, rubber bands armed with paper clips plucked across the room.

And I laughed through it all, had a rag of a time, until Dad showed up. After PTA meetings where I was held to account, Dad started popping up at school and sitting in on random classes. He never caught me mid-act, just sat in the back in his Clarks and slacks, looking on and embarrassing the fuck out of me. But it was not enough. I required more than I deserved. I had made it through Lemmel because my teachers blocked all other doors. They met, organized, double- and triple-teamed us, held us after school, pushed, prodded, until they obliterated job descriptions and fell somewhere between pastor, parent, and counselor. I could match passion with passion. But at Poly teaching was a job. Teachers did what was expected, and thought they could get the same. I demanded more of them, and virtually nothing of myself.

So this is how my first year in the royal city ended—handcuffed in the office of the school police. My second semester English teacher was a small man with a small voice. He was my last period, and talked with the sort of dead voice that bore down on my eyelids. I accorded him all the esteem of an anthill, and expected great deference in return. It was one of those spring afternoons at the end of the year, when all your hormones are fighting to break loose. But still, we had to stomach some boring zero prattling on about adverbs, clauses, and conjunctions. Who gives a fuck when you spent the whole day watching Tamara Garrett in tight jeans, and you know she's gonna be on the 44 bus, after school, her lush brown eyes dazzling all comers.

I walked into class in this state of mind, half looking for any way out. I stood at the front joking with a buddy, while all the other students took their seats. I was asked many times to sit down, until the teacher just lost his cool and sunned me in front of the whole class. I don't even remember what he said, but he'd raised his voice, and in front of a crowd, I could not back down.

I raised my hand and mushed him in the face. "Don't you ever yell at me again in your life."

He quietly ordered me outside, and then summoned the school police. And so hyped on ego and image was I that I mouthed so much to the officer that I was put in cuffs and escorted to his office where he prepared a report. I was suspended immediately, potentially expelled, and told not to return without a parent. I caught the 33 home by myself and that was when it all began to set in. All my life, I played my position. I was tired. Here was my declaration of borders and respect. But of course there was a price. And the merchant was my father.

He was waiting in the foyer at the door, again magically off work at the worst possible time. He was there with Ma and Jovett, half smiling through an awkward mix of shock and anger. Jovett walked out of the room and then it came. He threw an open hand and I hit the floor.

My mother stepped in.

Paul, Paul.

He shoved her away.

Woman, get off me.

And then he was swinging away, channeling a chi ancient as Equiano. The power was passed down from mothers guarding their sons from the lash, and later from the pyre, rope, and fat sheriff. My father swung with the power of an army of slaves in revolt. He swung like he was afraid, like the world was closing in and cornering him, like he was trying to save my life. I was upstairs crying myself to sleep, when they held a brief conference. The conference consisted of only one sentence that mattered—Cheryl, who would you rather do this: me or the police?

I saw my mother some hours later in our small kitchen. She tried to explain what she felt, but began to cry instead. She knew that I had no idea how close I was, would always be, to the edge, how easily boys like me were erased in absurd, impractical ways. One minute we were tossing snowballs at taxis, firing up in front the 7-Eleven, speeding down side streets and the next we're surrounded by unholstered guns, a false move away from going down. I would always be a false move away. I would always have the dagger at my throat.

This was the first time my parents pleaded me back into school. That night, we walked over to Mondawmin and ate at Long John Silver's. Our talk was regular. They held no debt. They met with the school principal to testify to my character. They met with my English teacher to assure him I was no threat. They met with the school police officer so that he knew there was no history of drug use. They met with a local magistrate to assure him there was no need for the State.

I returned a week later, and a few weeks later I was off to summer school. My mother took me over to archrival City College and wrote a check. After class, I'd come home—and a fresh box of books would greet me. I spent my weekends with the neighborhood boys. Every weekend night someone's mother—except mine—was off working the night shift. We'd gather at that unchaperoned house, dial up the jennys, throw on some club tapes, and sip from bottles until we were five steps beyond nice.

There I am outside Mondawmin Mall, bribing alcoholics into copping cheap fortified wine. I walk back to the anointed crib, bid my slaps of five, and pass out brown paper bags. An hour in, and I am floating, freaking some girl completely off beat. I wake up with bells ringing outside each of my temples and birds of pain circling overhead. I continue like this for months, until on a dare I down a forty of Red Bull solo, and spend a morning massaging the toilet bowl.

My parents never caught me like that, but they could see me running off the rails. Dad looked south to D.C., and called in old alliances formed years ago selling books at the Mecca. He contacted NationHouse, a coalition of brothers and sisters who, like my father, believed that the revolution could not be blustered into existence but must be built. Their group had purchased a building in the heart of the ravaged northwest of Washington, a command center from which they plotted the creation of a state within a state.

As in the Akan tradition, all their children were named according to days of their birth—Kofi for born on Friday, Kwaku for Wednesday. NationHouse flowered with Knowledge and culture—jazz recitals, spoken word, and regular lectures on our regal past and methods of return. They organized a school to educate their kids, sent them off for college credits at fourteen, and then for a bachelor's two years later. Everyone wore dashikis and lappas, kufis and head wraps. There were no perms.

Then, deep in the heart of Jeff Davis, in old Virginal, they purchased hallowed ground. The acres consecrated a century earlier through the toil of our mothers were the site of a great spiritual renewal. There was an unmarked slave graveyard, noticeable only by depressions in the land.

There was a path where Gabriel Prosser, all glory to him, had walked while planning his great slave rebellion, before the deceivers dropped dime.

One Sunday, my father packed me, Kier, Jovett, and Ma into the yellow and brown station wagon, and compared a white sheet of directions with his road atlas. It was hot August. Me and Kier had been remanded to Nation-House, and their plot of land. In the summer they ran a camp, in hopes of deprogramming kids from the lies of the great Satan. Dad drove down a long highway, till it connected to another highway, and that highway became a street, and that street turned into a narrow dirt road. The liberated acres were not formidable. What I saw was a big house presiding over sprawling fields, a valley, and forest. There was orientation and the completion of some forms, and then we were left there with our hooded sleeping bags, bug repellant, army surplus flashlights, and spare clothes.

We were not afraid, even though we knew no one. We arrived early, and shot hoops on a netless rim behind the house. All that Sunday, kids arrived until we had enough boys for fifty putout, then three on three. By then, I had learned that the rock and hoop were the king of icebreakers. All the other kids were camp vets, but by dinner we were joking and doing two-man military satire—Back in the war, you didn't have dinner. Someone passed you sticks and gruel, and you liked it.

I was teased those next two weeks, as always. Big, awkward, and still without a jump shot, I was too tempting a target. But I fell in with these kids in a way that I had fallen in with no one before. All of us knew why you abstained on the Fourth and the meaning of Nkrumah.

All our names were alien—Kwame, Jua, Ansentewaa—and traceable back to the continent of the originators. It was as if, on this holy plot of land, the revolution had come off and the world had been remade as the brothers envisioned it in '68. I lost myself there, felt confirmed and the freedom of being unoriginal.

We were forbidden to eat candy, cookies, and cakes. We were fed oatmeal in the morning, sandwiches for lunch, and groundnut stew in the evening. On Fridays they set us free with turkey hot dogs and potato chips. All the elders were addressed by the title Mama or Baba. We had to run a mile every morning, then shower, and participate in the day's ordained activities. We had free time, and played pickup football or three on three. We camped out and swapped off guard duty in the middle of the night.

I remember sitting in a small makeshift conference room on the first floor of the big house. It was film night, but our babas even invested this with meaning. We watched *Three the Hard Way* and giggled at the boom of Jim Brown's cannon compared with the pop-pop of his racist foes. The next night, we saw the film version of *The*

Spook Who Sat by the Door, Sam Greenlee's tale of black revolution. For the next hour, one of the babas led us in discussion. Was any of it plausible? What had we learned about the nature of white supremacy?

But most of us were occupied by smaller things. I was like any other fourteen-year-old boy, assaulted by internal chemistry and in the presence of jennys, subject to forgetting my name, address, and other vital information. Of course they were there, remanded from across the East Coast and regal in all their original blackness—dreads, braids, cornrows, short naturals, and head wraps for the two or three who'd foolishly permed. Kier scooped one right away, and these two spent the remainder of camp disappearing at random hours. I was, even in my newfound naturalness, profoundly still me—awkward and perpetually offbeat, crumbs in my hair, juice stains on my tee shirts. So I played my position and sought other outlets to deal with all the improper energy.

Toward the end of camp we were practicing for a final performance to be put on for our parents. There was to be a session of drumming and dancing, rhythms and moves imported from the west coast of Africa in the days when the Conscious folks thought the answers for all our problems lay in connections with back home. By then I was an

MC, and thus feeling that the marriage of beats and lyrics was a charter ship back to the Knowledge of the elder world. The current was powered by all the usual angst and alienation of this age. An hour, a pen, a pad and I was plugged in, the material plane falling away, and the world remade along the lines of my yearning imagination. In those years, hip-hop saved my life. I was still half alien to the people around me. I loved them, mostly because I'd realized that there was no other choice. Hip-hop gave me a common language, but that August, on liberated land, I found that there were other ways of speaking, a mother tongue that, no matter age, no matter interest, lived in us all.

The djembe is a drum, carved from wood. Its bottom is a wide outlet. If you trace its outline upward, you find the drum narrows until about halfway through its length. From there, it gradually blooms outward until, at its crown, it is as much as three times the size of its bottom. This crown is covered with the shaved skin of a goat. Rope running along the drum's side is tightened to effect a sharper sound. The drum is played with bare hands. Its sound varies from a piercing slap to a deep tonal moan and a barely inaudible bass. A djembe drummer is usually accompanied by a djun-djun player, the djun-djun being a giant bass drum played with a stick.

I was transfixed from first time I saw this combina-

tion. This is half true. At every affair throughout my childhood where my father sold books there was someone at
least playing a djembe, and some head-wrapped mama
singing the Swahili prayer "Funga Alafia." But my new
fascination corresponded to my age, I think, because the
djembe, the way it hangs between the legs, is virility itself
and has a special call to young boys looking for ways to express the change popping off inside. There was a boy playing. In his hands the drum sounded like a gun, if guns were
made to be music. The boy, only slightly older than me, af-
fixed it between his legs with the aid of a long strap, and
ever so casually began to make it sing. We were learning
the dance steps culled from the Mandé, the traditional gy-
rations made to heal the insane, celebrate the harvest, or inaugurate a tournament of wrestlers. I could not move. True
enough, the initial cause was great fear—everyone knew I
danced as awkwardly as I moved through life. But more so,
I was held by how the brother played, and how unconsciously it all came out. It was like he had no plans. I could
catch the basic beat, but what he brought out of it showed
that he heard more. And as I listened, I became bewitched.

The djun-djun held a steady rhythm, and the boy on
djembe would follow until the spirit got the best of him
and he was off on his own solo. He would beat out a series
of rhythms meant to match particular dance steps. The
drum had a sharp, piercing sound, and followed the heart-

beat of the djun-djun. It was like watching a great MC rhyme wordlessly, scatting almost, pulling new patterns and rhythms from the air. My breathing quickened whenever the drumming began. I would bob and nod unconsciously. My hands would move involuntarily.

And I was not even the hardest hit. On our last day we did our performance, a spirited bit of dancing and singing anthems that connected us to the Mother. At the end, we gathered with our smiling, proud parents. My mother told me I looked straightened out, slimmed down, and all in all more assured. I walked back to say my good-byes and found a group of kids circled around our dance instructor. She was a lovely woman with a short natural and glasses—a second wife, in the old Akan tradition, taken in with her young son by one of the community patriarchs.

She walked back and forth in a line, bouncing almost, her arms akimbo, her eyes rollicking wildly in their sockets. At her side stood her husband, who explained that the drums had called in the old deities and now one of them had taken her body as its own. She was now an oracle of sorts. Each of us approached individually and on our knees, and through the fog of tongues, we were each given a word of heeding in scattered English. None of this was planned. Our parents stayed back.

I did not understand, nor remember, what was said to me. I had no context for what I saw. I was raised godless, and in place of the One True, given a pantheon of ancestors, some direct, some in spirit, who had made my life, as it was, a possibility. I don't know, still don't know, if I believed the possession. Still, when the djembe called, I knew I had felt wild ecstatic energies coursing through me over which I lacked control. The thought of touching that sort of power, the direct current to the Motherland, sent me reeling. And as we drove home that Sunday night, through the Virginia darkland, I thought only of djembes. I had only drumming running through my head.

=====

CHAPTER 6

Float like gravity,
never had a cavity . . .

The babas dropped us off in the blackness, at the tip of Washington, D.C., Chocolate City, in the midst of late winter rain. Above, we heard cars screeching through puddles, water splashing off to the side. There were five of us, all told, five with names as heavy as my own—Ibrahim, Changamire, Banatunde, Kier—and me, the oldest, presumptive leader of this line. A week before, we were back in the liberated lands in Virginia, where they worked us all day, then made us spar outside with the older, bigger boys. I stood in my fighting stance, in the manner of our self-defense trainer, Baba Mike, my elbows bent, holding back my power right. But when they paired me off with big Kwaku, who'd crossed over the year before, all that technique went to the wind, and I was swinging for creation. He slapped me up for a good two minutes, which sounds short—but in a fight, it's enough time to put a mind out, or at least remove all its higher brain function. We were just sparring, but I don't think I even landed a jab. Still, afterward, they fed us fried chicken, biscuits, greens and built us all back up.

Now, it was breakdown time again. They'd dropped the five of us in the wild, charged us with finding our way back home. This was the last private ritual in our transition into manhood. We were still admonished for leering at girls, expected to live under the orders of our babas, and perform at the top of our class. But the world was opening fast upon us, and few among our generation had been prepared.

This was 1991. The mania was declining and the crack era was fading into a haze of stuffed White Owls and reconstructed Phillies. Still, at night the Enchantress appeared before my brothers and implored them to madness. They'd wake up the next morning, lumber down to the corner, the rec centers, the ball courts, talking up their parish's murder numbers, scheming on the murder capital's crown.

The righteous third were still marshalling their forces. Grandmothers rode up from the Carolinas, snatched boys off the street ear first and into flagging homes of worship. Uncles came home from Germany, Korea, and went upside knuckled heads. Banished fathers in their county blues pleaded on collect calls, across plastic dividers. Around my way, the great autodidacts and awesome seers—Dr. Ben, John Henrik Clarke, Asa Hilliard, Tony Browder, Marimba Ani—searched our history for any way out. What they sought were artifacts of culture that once kept us whole, relics of rituals lost to the Cataclysm. From their work, the elders of NationHouse emerged with the Great Rites, a series of labors meant to instill the warrior code in boys who would, always too soon, be men. Across the land, babas, like the ones at NationHouse, carried the ritual, until now, anywhere you find the Conscious, you find these ancient rites of redemption.

Every Saturday morning for six months, me and Kier came to NationHouse and were drilled on all the rudiments of what awaited. We started with self-defense and calisthenics at seven A.M. Then moved to elementary plumbing, history told from our side, and the cosmology of the Dogon. Later we learned the correct posture for firing a rifle. But I left the iron alone. Something about it never felt right. The end was enthronement in the House of Ankobia, Nation-House's fraternal order whose hierarchy and rituals were borrowed from ancient stately kingdoms. Among the Twi, the Ankobia were the standard-bearers, the vanguard of the people. I was senior on my line of boys, and thus handed the lead. The thought was that I would be a leader in deed, setting an example for my younger brothers. And though in theory, I believed in what was to be done, I half worked my way through the entire piece. During the week, I skipped calisthenics. I just barely memorized the Ankobia pledge. That was the old me. Even reborn, a part of me stayed in the old world where I was still a teenager and bucked authority like it was my job.

But I had made it to this final test. The night before our group of imminent Ankobites stayed at the home of an appointed elder. Kier and I played Super Nintendo until we were sent to bed. A few of the babas woke us only a few hours later, sent us to get dressed; and when we saw them next, they were in their winter coats, wiping no sleep from their eyes, clutching blindfolds, and guiding us out of the house and into the back of a van. The van would stop every twenty minutes. The door would slide open with a rusty crash, and under our blindfolds we could feel the seats pressing further down and buckling under the extra weight of additional boys. Under the overpass, we were hustled out onto a street, where we stood in a blind gaggle by the van. Baba Yao, one of the kindest of the elders, removed the blindfolds and returned to the driver's seat. He lowered the window.

Be back to NationHouse by dawn, he told us.

Then he drove off.

We stood there for a moment gathering our faculties and blinking in the dark. I was on alien land, a forty-minute ride out of Baltimore, but the D.C. boys figured things out quick. We were in Blackbyrd's woods, and to make dawn we had to get moving. Despite our slothful resistance, we'd been made fit by thousands of jumping jacks, and ably assumed a light running pace. It was dark almost the entire way. We did not talk much, except to complain, and guess which baba had come up with this stupid test, and how it had anything to do with Kemit, Kush, or Punt.

And then the babas's minions arrived, brothers who'd gone through the Rites the year before and now had their chance to give out some of the hardship they'd taken. We were jogging down Georgia Avenue, the main artery of black D.C., when we saw them pulling up in another mini-van. I think back on it now, and am amazed at how violence was everywhere, even in our theater. In their minds they were prepping us for some amorphous war. By now the

Conscious had come to grips with the nonrevolution but still clung to the hopeful thought that an army in waiting was needed for the moment when things turned.

The minions hopped out, threw up their hands, and started dancing like boxers. We went at it—right there in the street—no closed hands to the face, but everything else allowed. All I remember is the flailing limbs, half nelsons, and headlocks, and then the older brothers laughing and driving off. We picked ourselves up, kept moving.

The sun was just barely out when we got back. Baba Yao saluted us at the door and gave us black sweats, our medallions of initiation, then marched us inside.

That's as far as I can go. I haven't been Ankobia in years, can't recall a word of the pledge. But I honor what they did for me, the aim of those reclaimed rituals, and how they saved us from a savage time.

I was anchored. Against everything we saw, against all the wild stories of sisters turned night hags and brothers gone ronin, every Saturday morning we would drive to NationHouse and be greeted by a squadron of the unbroken who recalled the days of old splendor, of Nefertari, Askia, and Akhenaton, and instructed us to bring it back. On our shoulders they loaded a nation, and every elder who knew us believed we were prophetic, that we'd pull Celestia from the Nine Hells of Baator, that we'd bring sun and oceans to this wasteland.

It was a slow-acting drug. But through the years I came to know that in the galaxy of DuBois and Booker T., of Cheryl Waters and Paul Coates, of Mama Makini and Baba Jules, my errors were never borne solo, my accolades were never mine alone. So many of us had turned to henchmen and mercenaries. Whether bourgeoisie in Woodlawn or thugging in Flaghouse, niggers were acting like it could not happen, like their lives were only theirs alone. But the Rites were a great web tying me to all my people in all times, from West Baltimore to Dakar, from Mondawmin across the haunted waves to Gorée.

The Ankobia elders brought us back the next week for a public entrance into the world of men. We were swaddled in all white and each handed a spear. In age order, we were led out through the broken streets of Chocolate City, but wherever we walked the concrete shifted, glowed, and healed. The stunned community turned to the processional, which wasn't just the newly minted men I was with but all of Ankobia's mamas and babas and the girls too, our counterparts, who'd undergone their own private rites. In these darkening years, even the Unconscious had some sense that things had gone bad, and thus they took anything upright among children as a righteous step. So the old heads on the corner, the mothers with their heads under scarves, they all smiled and clapped as we walked past silently, even if they knew nothing about what we were.

157

Ankobia rented out a middle school cafeteria for our final ceremony. We walked in, and family and friends stood in ovation, spines of the great web. We were introduced by name and accomplishment. We recited our pledge, holding spears aloft. But I did not come completely into focus until I heard the djembes. It was like a girl you'd seen once, exchanged everything but numbers and had been plotting on for weeks. In our final days we learned a sacred dance that we performed with the drums. But hearing it there, watching big Kwaku go off and the crowd clap and cheer, I was entranced.

Mornings I'd wake up with old rhythms in my head, drum patterns that I could not even name. My mother saw no future for me in drumming. But still it was one of my parents' approved activities, the sort of thing that would further strengthen my bond with the community. My time with my folk was close to the end. I was the last of a group of Dad's children born into uncertain times. We were poorly planned for and chaotically conceived. In two years they would see me off, and turn their attentions to Menelik, eight years my junior, whose only great concerns were dinosaurs and the cycles of active volcanoes.

I saw it coming. That fall, Dad drove us down Liberty Heights until it became Liberty Road and the streetlights became less frequent. There, up a forested hill with houses tucked in the right side, he revealed our new manse on

Campfield Road. It was astonishing. Six bedrooms, a breeze-way, garage, barn, grassy acreage so sprawling that you'd need a tractor to keep it in shape. It was Barrington Road and more, a haven out in the county near enchanted woods. I should have been relieved, struck that the great horror ini-tiated with the snatch of a skullcap was now at end. But I was old school like Charlie Mack and Ready C. I had made my home among an alien Tioga, had learned the customs, made it native to me, earned my colors so wherever I walked if I wasn't Little Melvin, I was West Baltimore all the same.

And there was politics. For years, we'd held out against the scourge, like the last lost platoon, and now we were folding our red, black, and green in retreat.

I took it to my father. He was seated in the basement of Tioga, and all around were shelves of books. Two steel desks were jammed together, with invoices and paperwork scattered on top. I told him of my concerns, that there were—ideals at stake, principles in living where the strug-gle was, in never moving or giving up.

This is what I said. But underneath was also the fact that I'd become proud that Mondawmin, with all its allure of danger, was my backyard. That I survived it daily and could raise my hand when anyone yelled *Is West Baltimore in the house?* Maybe Dad heard that in my protest, because he just listened and nodded, did not offer a counter, just leaned back and took it in. When I was done, he lowered his head until he was looking above his reading glasses and spoke.

Son, all my life I've lived among the people. I've lived in cramped quarters since I was born. I am forty-four. I have never had a big yard.

He caught me flush with that one. I thought my science triumphant; I knew I had no answer for all his years. I had never been evicted. My house was strange, but none of my brothers doubled as cousins, and I had never tangled with the gangs of North Philly. My dad had come up among a sort of mayhem. They were at war. That was all. So in the autumn we moved north, and I was left wondering what it all—Lemmel, Mondawmin, the Great Rites— had been worth. Just as soon as I dropped anchor I was afloat again.

But I got my drum, a dark brown djembe with a wide mouth and rich, deep sound. At first I took a Saturday train to Chocolate City for lessons, and practiced alone during the week. I got nowhere. A natural can pull from a simple palette of sound and paint you the universe. His technique is to ride out with his brother drummers, then at the ordained moment take the lead and find rhythm where others hear none. But when I touched my drum there was nothing but a muddy, plodding groan. I spent six months like that, traveling to D.C. for lessons and coming back with only a murmur for a sound. After school, I'd practice out in the breezeway, desperately trying to play anything distinct. But all I got back was that old dirty rumble.

There was drumming in Baltimore, too, and I banded with the Sankofa Dance Theater. In the heyday of the movement '60s, my elders reached back for anything original they could grab—plantain, kufis, a new name. Then they saw gorgeous West African ballets, with their fervid dancing and drumming, and knew that the tradition had to be brought to the other side. They founded dance companies with names taken from Swahili. They convened at megashows in which each of them would perform in successive order. It became a religion of sorts, like hip-hop, or football down south. My parents saw me embracing the reclaimed culture and it filled them with hope.

That year, I drummed with some brothers from Sankofa. My technique was still invisible, but the events of the day outstripped personal concerns. We were in a church. My old friend Salim's father had died. We were the sort of boys who were close at a young age, who played together and slept over, whose parents would babysit the others' children, and then for reasons that are never explained to kids, just drifted apart. His mother, Mama Kabibi, was a beautiful dancer, who'd founded the Sankofa Dance Theater, and I remembered his father as healthy and robust.

But when I last saw him at a Sankofa drumming class, he was depleted, and thin, a victim of years of HIV, which was roiling all of Baltimore.

He had fallen, like so many fathers of that time, and in his place had stepped another, Baba Kauna, who took up with Mama Kabibi and assumed the four kids who were left behind. When he picked up the sword, Baba Kauna became mythical to us, much like my own father, so much so that we simply addressed him as Baba. His new charge, Salim, was golden and at thirteen could make a drum do things that a lifetime in Senegal would not teach. He led Sankofa's drum squad with another sun child, Menes, and always they subtly competed to see whose hands would carry the day.

They were not supposed to be Sankofa's lead drummers. But every time an older god was brought in to take the reins, he'd give it a few months and then fade out. And so the drumming was handed over to the kids. I played with them at the funeral for Salim's father, and immediately felt a bond that went beyond the actual drumming. Later, as I played more with them, as my hands were cleaned, I came to understand what was between us. We'd come up much the same way, raised with the same traditions, abhorrence of pork and the Fourth of July. Here, like Ankobia, was a place where I need not explain my name. So

I joined up, and in that I mean I simply made myself a regular, and though still I had hands of stone, they took me on as one of their own.

Back at the Mecca, Big Bill spent more time managing his herb stash than his accumulating studies. He was completely unprepared. He'd been dragged through his school years by parents, and the occasional teacher with whom he shared some mutual interest beyond the syllabus. But the study-sense that by then was natural to so many students was nowhere within him, and now unmoored and unchained from Dad's discipline, he was free to indulge all the hedonism his parents had kept at bay.

By second semester he'd assembled a collection of brothers who reflected the old West Baltimore values of loyalty and furious fists. All around him were people swimming in light, rising above the plagues that afflicted the untalented 90 percent. They were fifth-generation black bourgeoisie, project prodigies straight out Cabrini, Merit scholars waving off Harvard, progeny of black flight starving for a cocoon of their own kind. And while big trumpets heralded our Fall, these kids presented beats and rhymes to let the world know that the struggle was epic and continued, that the strugglers were immortal. Slowly Bill was creeping up on Consciousness again, seemed on the verge of awakening, but mostly he was trapped in the smaller war, the skirmish for identity and respect.

His weekend nights were aimless. He would sit up drinking with his New York homeys, David and Mitch, and spark up a session. One night it was all dying down. David called his girlfriend and a dude picked up the phone. Everyone was hot with liquor, and in the background Bill and Mitch started blowing up this kid's head, goading him and pushing him deeper until he ended the phone call with a Nigger I'm on my way, you better not even be in the same hemisphere when I step up.

David gets off the phone. He is not a big or foolish man, and, if left solo, it would have died there. Words thrown into the air, while better sense prevails. Already he is shrinking back. But Bill and Mitch are in his ear, breaking out with the Nigger represent, and You ain't no punk, inflating him until they are piling into David's car and heading to his girlfriend's dorm.

In those days, the Howard Plaza Towers were hot. Dorms built in the style of apartments, they had kitchens, private bathrooms, and sleeping quarters. Outside there was a small plaza, and on weekends Howard students, drawn by the air of lush life, would assemble along the shallow wall, milling and waiting on mischief. Bill and his two friends parked out front, and beelined through the plaza, shit-talking the whole way. They flashed their ID to security and took the elevator up. Of course the dude was a man in his own right and was there waiting, and also more than what they'd pictured in all their big talk and ego.

Nigger, he was stacked like Tony Atlas, I'm talking circa '76, with the Q-Dog brand on his shoulder. He was down with the Omegas, known as an order of enlightened thugs and collegiate brawlers.

David shrank back at the size of his opposition, and the Greek talisman burned into his flesh, which meant that help was always and already en route. He slipped into double-talk, got to stuttering, and light in his voice. Bill was in the back, shaking his head, and for the honor of his small unknown clan, he stepped up. At first he tried defusion, but the ruckus had recruited instigators and other boys who couldn't find a party that night or had struck out with some chick. I told you Big Bill was rarely scared, would not back down, and now faced off, not even with the original adversary but just some other kid who wandered in thinking a brawl would make his Friday complete.

They took it outside, but by now phone calls had been placed, and the opposition was deep, hopping out of Cherokees and removing their jewels. Bill and his crew were surrounded in the plaza, three against the horde, when Mitch yelled to Bill—Yo, end this. Bill reached in his dip, untucked the iron, and shot into the air.

All the plaza scattered, ducked, screamed—Nigger's shooting. One brave one adjusted his cape and stepped up.

Mutherfucker, you ain't shooting shit. You ain't shooting a mutherfucking thing.

Bill brought the gat level with his shoulder. Nigger, if you don't back up right now, I'ma bust you in your mutherfucking chest.

Brain chemicals kicked in, and the kid backed off, and by then Howard security had showed, just one rent-a-cop, but it was now all real.

Young man, put down the gun. Put down the gun, please.

I'm not putting shit down. I'm not putting nothing down.

Young man, please put down the gun. I'm not going to ask you again.

It was then that Bill recovered some of himself. He put the .38 on the ground. The cop approached and grabbed his arm. Bill pointed at some of his former combatants, now across the street watching, and yelled out—What about them?

The cop looked over, and Bill jerked his arm free, broke out. He darted across Banneker field, icy in winter, and then ran through the darkness to the apartment my two sisters shared. He spent the night on the floor. The next morning Mitch and David came through with clothes.

That was when he found out—the chick wasn't even David's girlfriend, just someone he'd claimed and talked big about.

The stupidity of it all hit Bill square in the face. Here he was at the great capstone of all Negro education, and on a jenny he barely even knew he had placed his life. That shook him. He could not analyze it all. He did not know what this meant about where he should be bound for next. But he knew that the old ways, the old customs and styles of being, the Knowledge which had saved him, steeled him against the scourge, could not help him here. This was not Murphy Homes. He was in another world. He was playing by alien rules.

At home, I struggled through Poly. The spell of the enchanted city had now worn off. After summer school, I spent the year flailing again. I look back now, and I know something had to be wrong. I could not sit still without talking. I could not concentrate longer than fifteen minutes. In class I'd watch the clock until I fell asleep or spend the entire period working on rap lyrics. My head was Penn Station, and every half hour a train arrived dropping off a new batch of thoughts and possibilities, pushing out everything else that was old.

By then Kier was at Poly, too, and inserting himself

into the mix. Halfway into the year, someone popped his lock and made off with his hooded Raiders Starter. I caught up to Kier in the hallway, punching his fist into his palm. Somebody had to take a loss. By the end of the day he'd assembled his crew. I was there, laughing with a group of other knuckleheads, egging Kier on.

We stood on the number 33 bus stop, brazenly in front of the school. Across the way were two white kids, one in a red Chiefs Starter, the other in one from the Raiders. It was not their whiteness that marked them, so much as the fact that their whiteness made them a minority in this part of Baltimore, and thus unlikely to have a sizable team that could hit back. We hyped Kier up—Nigger, you ain't going do shit. He raised his eyebrows. Bet. Then ran across the street.

Yo, can I see that? Can I see that jacket? Yo, that look like mine. Yo, where'd you get that from?

And then he was swinging at the kid in the Raiders jacket. The kid's friend backed off, like he wanted no part. I stood across the street stupidly laughing with the rest of them. It was all another mask. Inside, I felt flashbacks to my year of terror. But I would not let it show here. Better to move with the sentiment of the crowd and act like I never caught the Rodney King myself.

I failed three classes that year. I got a letter of exile from the magical city. In the old days, Dad would have gone straight for the belt. But I was almost sixteen, and he was counting on the lessons kicking in, the books, the work, the bees and wax, the Ankobia initiation, the Rites, the Knowledge, Consciousness. He was waiting for me to finally police myself. He only looked at me after he saw the report card and shook his head.

I knew I was humiliating everyone I loved. They believed I was different and boundless, that when I looked out on a summer street, I may not have seen what was needed, what was the essence of survival, but what I saw was special and unique. They watched me absorb books about my own, and further, about foreign places and geographies. They knew I'd taught my brother Menelik the theory of the big bang. They believed I was a curious boy. And yet whenever someone threatened to put a grade on it, I fell asleep and lost interest.

In this, Big Bill and I were one. Our folks understood that there was war upon us and that school was a weapon that outdid any Glock. Yet the whole process—with its equally spaced desks, precisely timed periods and lectures, with its standardized pencils and tests—felt unnatural to me. But much as I hated their terms, having been impressed into them, I hated more the failing. So I was left with a great unconscious sadness, an emptiness which, even when I was alone, I was not fully aware. But it worked on me like an invisible weight, altered my laughter, posture, my approach to girls. Fuck what you have heard or what you have seen in your son. He may lie about homework and laugh when the teacher calls home. He may curse his teacher, propose arson for the whole public system. But inside is the same sense that was in me. None of us ever want to fail. None of us want to be unworthy, to not measure up.

My parents could not bank on this, but I was their son, and they were bound to do all they could on my behalf. Dad got real short with the words, but my mother still talked. I remember her pissed as hell that summer, having to cut another check for makeup classes. Still in all we'd be riding down Liberty, and in the midst of another lecture she'd get silent for a second and then start quoting Bob: Emancipate yourself from mental slavery, none but ourselves can free our mind. She fought to the end so I'd have my shot to do just that. My mother appealed my expulsion to the dean of Poly, stressed my virtues and their belief that someday soon, I would decide to be more than my grades had shown. I was a lucky child, and while in small things I caught a series of bad ones, in the epic sweep, time was on my side. The dean was new, had his own thoughts of reforming Poly so that it stood up to its epic tradition. He began with an act of mercy, waved his hands, and my transcript was spared.

I came back that year resolved to make Daniel Hale manifest. I'd been saved from exile, and for all my antics, I still believed in the Poly name, knew in some sense that this was more opportunity than most of the brethren received. I could not conceive laughing that off. I thought of improving my grades enough to qualify for football in my senior year. I started hitting the school gym with some friends. I only failed one class my first quarter—it was my best quarter since Lemmel.

Months earlier, my father left his job at the Mecca. That was the year he took me to see *Boyz n the Hood*, the touchstone film of our time and manifesto of endangered hominids the world over. Dad had spent the past ten years moving between the Press and his full-time job. The two complemented each other, and through the collections of the Moorland-Spingarn library he lived with a wealth of forgotten arcana, turn-of-the-century pamphlets, the papers of forgotten mystics. But his love was the Press, and for the first time ever, he had built enough to consider making his love his sole income. He gave me a say in his decision. If he left, my brother would still have tuition guaranteed, but since I hadn't been admitted, my free ride to the Mecca would evaporate.

He sat me down and made sure I understood the consequences. Son, he told me, if I leave, you're on your own. You've not been a great student. If I leave, you'll have to find your own way in, and I don't know how much of your schooling we can pay for.

I don't know how much of what I said affected anything. But even as my grades improved, inside I felt the True Me waiting. I did not want my father tied to that. He left later that year, and began living his dream. He was more of a presence in my school life, and his proximity was just more reason to improve my grades. I was still, as always, scared silly of him. Once I was beefing with my shop teacher over the sort of thing that really boils down to my small right to talk back. Still, it was enough that when I walked past him and bumped into his arm, he cried assault. I was sent to the office. I'd already been suspended for assaulting a teacher in my freshman year. The disciplining principal Mr. Brown, a brother who was well regarded by the kids, explained that I had a mandatory suspension in store, and called my father up to school.

He showed up with that perpetual grim look on his brown face, and I had no idea what torment he had in store. But before he could hatch his plot, he was taken aside by Mr. Brown and they spoke outside of my earshot. On the way home, Dad addressed me in a manner so unthreatening that I was certain it was some sort of verbal trap. I was big by then—over six feet and about 180 pounds, but my awkwardness remained. Was like my brain had not grown into the body, and whereas before my clumsiness was limited, I was now a threat to more than just the pitcher of juice on the table.

Son, you're growing into a big man. You're going to

have to be more conscious of yourself. You are not a mean kid, but because of your size you will do things that will be seen as a threat. You need to be conscious especially around white people. You are big, and you are a young black man. You need to be careful about what you do and what you say.

I spent the next three days at home, working for the Press but unpunished. I could feel us entering our last stages together. My parents were reaching the limits of their ability to impose their will, which always had been anchored by a physical threat. But Dad believed in the animal nature of us all, that at a certain age the boy becomes man, must be addressed as such, and then pushed out. I was raised with that understanding, with the sense that closer I got to the blessed number eighteen, the more my folks would pull back in preparation for my great ushering into the world.

I thought that this was how everyone came up, and those who did not were not worth consideration. I had no skills, and in the one thing all children are judged upon— school—I had always disappointed. Still, I had that ignorant confidence derived from the encouragement of mothers. I had no idea how I could do it, but the thought of my parents retreating was love to me, was admission that my independent time was approaching.

They were changing too. They were always smart, and kept their arguments mostly hidden from public view.

Still, I noted that each of them would disappear for days at a time. My mother would call and check in. Dad would explain that she was taking a break. I put nothing into it. I had so little by which to gauge their marriage. Most of my friends' parents were single, but what struck me more were the legion of fathers on the lam. From my own father, I got the picture that people meet all the time, think they're in love, and then it just goes bad. But I esteemed my father so much, even at odds with him as I was constantly, that I could not see anything else.

I was making my way through school, not quite up to standard but better than ever before. I paid attention in my math classes, made an honest stab at homework. After class was out I'd hit the gym and then the track. In March I did a few days of spring football practice, in anticipation of trying out my senior year. I was turning the corner, and I might have made it around, if it all hadn't come out.

These things are always so stupid when armed with hindsight, but in the moment it seems like all your existence converges in a moment, is out there on the table, and your options are limited. This day, I had a paper due. It was finished but late, and my entire English grade was held in the balance of getting it in. I was in my history class, a period before lunch, when it happened. My teacher was Mr. Stoddard, the sort of liberal white guy who showed us Ken Burns's *Civil War* and took a whole period to discuss the impact of Rodney King. I was a fan, and took great pleasure in our back-and-forth. This morning, we were debating the morality of the American Army and the recently concluded Desert Storm. Most of the class went with the country and argued for both. But I was black as Edmondson Avenue and AFRAM, and stood my solo ground. I wouldn't fight in any American Army against anyone close to my color.

What came next must have been simple clowning, the sort of comment a kid would yell out because he had nothing to offer except the possibility of sparking a good laugh. When I said I would not fight for America, skinny Shawn yelled from the back—

That's cause you a punk.

He got no laughter, but I felt an old burning in my chest. No one at Poly had ever said anything like that to me. I'd been tested a couple times, but I'd learned how to walk, when to smile, not talk too much, and though I lacked an ill pedigree, I still looked like a kid who knew the rules. I turned around, at the time not knowing who said what, and yelled in typical sixteen-year-old fashion—

Whoever said that ain't going say it to my face.

The class was absorbed by all the instigating ooohs, and Mr. Stoddard took control and calmed everyone down. But after class my nigger Brady told me it was Shawn who'd made the crack, and this made it worse. He was out of Fallstaff, the softest middle school in the city, where in my hated weaker days, I'd thought I wanted to attend. Shawn was a joker to me, would sit in the back of the class with a stupid grin, dressed like Kwamé. Whatever, I told Brady. Shawn don't want nothing to do with me.

But a few minutes later, Brady returned, hyping up the whole affair, Yo, Shawn said he want to see you. He said you could see him in the bathroom right outside the cafeteria at lunch.

I walked down with five or six other boys, all hyped on my own scent, and found him standing there with his best friend, Tyrone. I started barking soon as I walked.

Nigger, you wanna see me? You got something you wanna say to me, mutherfucker? What's up, nigger? What's up?

He was not so much afraid as stunned by the vehemence of things. We had never beefed before, and here I was off, one inane comment escalating and lobbying for war. Neither of us was built like that, the exploding of fists was unnatural to us, only adopted when it was felt that something precious was at stake. But I was of my time, and this was it. Painfully I'd come to know that face must be held against everything, that flagrant dishonor follows you, haunting every handshake with all your niggers, disputing every advance on a jenny. Shawn was, at first, true to his better nature, and backed down and held up open hands.

But I'd come too far to be gracious. I stuck my finger in his grill—

That's right. 'Cause you a bitch-ass nigger.

—and walked out.

Nowadays, I cut on the tube and see the dumbfounded looks, when over some minor violation of name and respect, a black boy is found leaking on the street. The anchors shake their heads. The activists give their stupid speeches, praising mythical days when all disputes were handled down at Ray's Gym. Politicians step up to the mic, claim the young have gone mad, their brains infected, and turned superpredator. Fuck you all who've ever spoken so foolishly, who've opened your mouths like we don't know what this is. We have read the books you own, the scorecards you keep—done the math and emerged prophetic. We know how we will die—with cousins in double murder suicides, in wars that are mere theory to you, convalescing in hospitals, slowly choked out by angina and cholesterol. We are the walking lowest rung, and all that stands between us and beast, between us and the local zoo, is respect, the respect you take as natural as sugar and shit. We know what we are, that we walk like we are not long for this world, that this world has never longed for us.

I was sitting at the lunch table, shooting that Shawn ain't shit, when he ran out, and wiped my memory. Who knows what his boy told him in that bathroom after we left, what stories and taunts he used to hype him into frenzy? What he knew was that something had been stolen from him, not by the local badass but some kid in contacts who was barely king of himself. Later, they told me he ran out screaming, the steel trash can above his head, and when it landed it boomed so loud that the whole cafeteria turned. That I crumpled to the white bench, and said nothing. That he dropped the can, held his hands over his head like Sweet Pea Whitaker, and started to dance. That he was off in a dreamworld, his honor restored, and my own stolen, added to his. That his back was turned when I rose up, and unfurled the green David Banner. That I grabbed him from behind, slammed him onto the white tabletop, and climbed up.

That was when I returned to myself, and what I felt was not pain but a sick power. What I wanted was to banish this kid to the prosthetics ward, to turn his whole grill piece into a project for surgeons. I pinned him on top of the table and swung with both hands. To the right I saw one of Kier's old girls yelling—Ta-Nehisi, Ta-Nehisi! Stop! But I was time traveling back to the days at Lemmel and all the razors I'd swallowed for ignorance of rules. Now it all flew back out, and though I was aware, I felt an enveloping rage, as my hands were lifted from the controls.

I was pulled back by two of my more responsible friends who were above the howling and instigation. I touched the side of my face and saw red on fingers.

Yo, what did he hit me with? What the fuck did he throw at me? A juice?

Naw, man, he hit you with a trash can.

I'ma kill that nigger.

I started rushing back his way, but they grabbed me and took me up to the office. I was a mess. Vice principals and secretaries gasped. Someone called the ambulance. My buddies got early dismissal. There was blood all over their clothes. Dad met me at the hospital.

He was about as comforting as I can ever remember him in all our time in that house, which meant asking if I was okay and not saying much on the ride home. But I didn't need comfort. I felt, for the first time, what I wished I had felt years ago, that someone had tried to take something from me, that he'd attempted to reduce me to a status below my station. And that I didn't let it happen.

I came back the next day, staples in my head, but not to laughter and taunts. They said I was the brown bomber, that they'd never seen a nigger lose it like that, and to top it off, Shawn—not me—had been expelled from school. I reveled for a week. Jennys from freshman year stepped to me, flush with vapors, and I was king until I started rifling through my backpack. My English paper was gone. I had lost it in the commotion.

That year, I tried to turn it around. But everything caught up with me. All my past failures from years before heaped onto my two assaults on teachers, to my fight in the cafeteria, and to my failing of English, and I was banished for good. My parents could not intercede here. My father was sitting in the living room on our gray sectional couch, and this is how I knew it was over. He wasn't even angry. He just sat there blank and went into a speech from which I only remember one line—

Ta-Nehisi, you are a disgrace to this family's name.

That hurt, and not because, before my father, mostly Coates had meant alcoholic, and orphaned kids. Because my father was Superman, the dude who pushed through Murphy Homes in search of Bill, the cat who was dealt a hand of seven kids by four women, and did his best to carry it, and I had completely let him down. But more than that was how I'd failed myself. No matter what the professional talkers tell you, I never met a black boy who wanted to fail.

As for Dad, of course he was always more complicated than what I allowed myself to see. He wore no cape and had his own questions to grapple with. This I was coming to know.

Months earlier I'd seen him sitting outside the office

with Jovett in her maroon Saturn. It was dark winter, and I was coming home from school. I approached and was greeted without nervousness or alarm. But I knew my father, and could feel that, in the way they were sitting there, that evening, there was something that I had not been told.

===

CHAPTER 7

Bamboo earrings, at least two pair

You may note that all my references to girls have been brief, and mostly touched by failure. My catalog was comic.

Page one: I sat on a fence in early June 1985, my last years of boyhood drawing to dark. I was waiting on Brenda Neil, who I knew had to walk this way to make it home. Soon, she'd be off to Fallstaff, or one of those boarding schools way out with horses and fencing teams. Of course, she was brown and lovely, her eyes were great planets, but what I remember most was how the world would pause and come to her, how she spoke and walked easily, like fifth grade, with all its giant uncertainties, was just her personal ballet. When she laughed, her voice lightly cracked, and with it something inside me, too, took days to set right. She would tap her number two pencil against a desk and look up and away for an answer, and even that dumb look thrilled me. Then I knew how the damned dinosaurs died, that even here, in Miss Boone's ordinary classroom, cataclysm awaits.

I was on the fence at Cold Spring and Callaway, a block away from the 7-Eleven where I saw my first gat, across the street from where the highwaymen of Wabash snatched my black skullie, sat there nursing my last chance. I don't remember what I said, but in response she walked past and would have smiled and said something nice, because she was not the type to get loud on you, and for now had rejected the seductive venom and back talk that is the birthright of all black girls. What I know is that I did not say what was needed, what ached beneath every rib, that I watched her walk away with, at best, good-bye and good luck.

I was born under a lame sign. Big Bill could make them yell, Go, William, and do the whop. Dad had his flock and thus direct evidence that, in these matters, his was the arm of Thor. But I had taken a wrong exit, picked up a manual written in French, because, in truth, my greatest disaster was that I just did not understand. Jennifer would clip me in the hallway, pull my shirt, punch me in the shoulder, grab at my chair while I reared back on two legs, mash an index finger in my face, then an hour later smile and ask what I was reading. But it never got through.

Page 7: There I am at my seventh-grade locker, half-way through the year of all hell. Teyanda whispers in my ear, Ta-Nehisi, I have a crush on you. I turn and she's running off, only to turn back for a second, unsmiling through her glasses, and say, It's true. I am overcome, but still I demand parted clouds and a booming voice. A glad-to-see-you grin would have helped, and furthermore I am not sure what I am supposed to do next. I could walk her home, but Teyanda lives down near Longwood where legionnaires carry war hammers and long daggers in their dip. I am my own quagmire, and so at the end of the week Teyanda extends her right hand to mush my face and sucks her teeth. Ta-Nehisi, I don't have a crush on you.

I should have known—all of us were damaged goods, and if I missed something it was this: My greatest perils were sudden and defined—a Timberland boot to the dome, the talking end of a three-eighty, a cop looking to make his night. But on the other side, the pitfalls were bottomless. This was the era of high schools fitted with nurseries; HIV was the air. Nigger, that year at Woodlawn, I had a mother or an expecting in every class. And still fools had the nerve to yell, You got a phat ass! from the passenger seat—always the passenger seat—of speeding cars, to sidle up and ask why you never smile. Who knew what this dude was holding behind those cold hazel eyes? Girls of Knowledge would shoot a nigger down without so much as eye contact, because they knew every smile, every infatuated act compromised security and handed us a weapon that we would only deploy for selfish use. So they made themselves into fortresses, and demanded you drop your arms before they even thought about the drawbridge. They had so much more to lose.

Page 12: It is 1992, and I am doing what I have mastered at Woodlawn—sleeping through health class, my head resting on folded arms, folded arms resting on my desk, next to one of Dad's latest reprints, which, needless to say, was not the text of the class. Ebony Kelly walked by with a stack of papers and tapped and tapped my desk until I came out of the haze. I was an exile then from Poly, banished from the crystal city and denied even the rep of a West Baltimore public school. What karmic poetry—I had spent all those years wrestling with the Knowledge only to become a county boy. I had disgraced my parents, and exhausted by the rigors of it all, they simply threw up their hands and backed off.

You do what you want, boy, Dad told me one day in

the car. But at the end of this school year, you will leave my house. You can go into the army, I don't care. But you will not be here next year.

Dad and Ma believed seventeen was an internship to manhood, that at that point, the child would be what he was. This was my senior year, the first time no one checked my homework, asked if I had studied, or requested progress reports from school. I came in with a 1.8 GPA. College would require a series of awesome labors. I would have to start with the invention of time travel. Still, I was blessed with some understanding of standardized tests, and thus SAT scores that, at least in Baltimore, stood out. And my advanced classes at Poly had softened my landing here in my senior year at Woodlawn. I had three classes after lunch— health, Spanish I, applied math. I showed my respect by sleeping as much as I could and pulling Bs on pop quizzes. The classrooms were crowded and tight. The last thing a teacher wanted was to make me into an issue. They left me to my afternoon nap. I left them to their restless kids.

Ebony had not been informed of the arrangement. She sat at the front of the class, knew all the answers, and was first pick for class errands. She tapped on the desk until I looked up, handed me some inane ditto, then picked up the thin book lying next to my arm.

What are you reading?

David Walker's Appeal. It's written by a black guy from the slavery days. He predicted a lot of the stuff they said in the '60s. They killed him, of course.

She stood there for a few moments, asking more about the book, then gave her impressions of Malcolm's memoirs and carelessly smiled. That was when I noticed her.

I came to Woodlawn not sure of what was next. Half of me saw myself fulfilling the destiny of those my mother called out as If-I-hadda-had-my-gun niggers. They stood on their corners, their brains otherwise correct, spewing tales of life-altering moments, conflicts which it all hinged on. But they come out losers, and the frame was always the same—If I hadda had my gun, that nigger wouldn't have said shit or If I hadda had my gun, that bitch would have let me see my kids.

It was taxonomy for losers, brothers who wasted their minds. That possibility, membership in a garbage heap of lost men, hung over me, clouding even my most primal impulses.

But she was black and beautiful like her name, and, wrong as it was, this made her prominent to me. Years ago I had embarrassed my mother. We were sitting with one of her girlfriends in a living room, and now came that predictable moment that I hated. Why do women care so much about the budding romances of young boys?

Girlfriend: Ta-Nehisi, what sort of girls do you like?

Ta-Nehisi: I like light-skin girls.

There must have been a gasp, but I was young and must have missed it, because my next image is postconversation, sitting in the car with my mother staring at me, the car unstarted. Her eyes were power drills, and though she herself was a shade from yellow, she was a patriot of a broader Africa.

Little boy, don't you ever say anything like that again. You can have your little eyes on whoever you want, for whatever you want. But you remember that these little black girls are somebody's daughter, somebody's sister— your sister, and someday, somebody's mother, and when it comes down, the white man won't take time to make distinctions. You need to check yourself, little boy.

I didn't get it right away, was even angry at first, but then days piled on to weeks and then on to months, until a shame came over me, and I understood. So by now I knew that "you're pretty for dark-skin girl" was a hate crime that Ebony probably had to fend off before. We talked reading and politics until the teacher sat her down, and throughout it all she smiled and giggled, and for the first time since

Callaway, I was down with someone who was both Knowledged and free.

I watched her in the halls over the following days. I was down with no one here. I talked little out here in the county school—I didn't even fuck with bucolia like that. I fed myself on my own myth. They were Snap to my Chill Rob G. I was the West Baltimore original, while they just played the part. But their girls, with their wrap skirts, sundresses, and wide-leg jeans, were exotica. She was a duchess among them. She stood out amid the dime pack—the ones who got their hair done monthly and touch-ups on the midweeks. She wore it wrapped or all pulled back into a French roll with blue glitter or curly bangs hanging down the front. They dressed like it was all a fashion show. They dispensed smiles and laughter, as if from a box of exquisite chocolates, with none to spare. All of them except Ebony. She was always laughing.

And she was Conscious. She was president of the cultural enrichment club, a black student union, but in deference to Woodlawn's nonblack 30 percent, no one called it that. I started going to meetings, mostly still just playing the back but occasionally piping up to interject a minor suggestion. We became closer this way, began to talk after health class or at the public library after school. I got the math in my usual, flicted way. Sidled with homework help, which of course, I did not need. I just wanted to see her alone, where all the grinning would belong to me.

In the dance studio, the sound of my djembe was forming.

That year, with all the adult drummers gone, we held it together.

After classes, I'd take my djembe out into the garage and practice until my muddy sound was cleaned. It was not the song of morning birds but still clearer than that old muffled groan. And I got better as the year went on, until finally I could play my own solos and lead the dancers in class down the floor.

Nothing short of religion can explain the molten feeling I derived from it all. Amid my failure and sudden parental abandonment, drumming was like a séance, a very loud séance—the drums, song, and dance whipped us into fury. You could hear us yelling over the roar as the currents of older gods rolled over us, and when fully on, we played in such unity that we were joined—all of us played our own part with our own sound, but we were one.

At night I went further, soaking goatskins in my parents' basement and shaving off the hair. I'd place them between three rings and affix this tightly to the top of a wooden djembe shell. With mountain-climbing rope, I'd tie the top rings to a smaller ring at the drum's belly and give it a day to dry. Then the next night I'd pull the rope with a stick and pliers until the skin was so tight over the drum that it felt like wood, and when you tapped it, the chained undead wailed out from under the Atlantic.

I had never done anything like this before. At first it all looked so impossible, and now that I'd been washed and baptized, drum solos I once marveled at now looked like three-year-olds banging at buckets. Then there were the djembes themselves. I built them not by parental edict, not under threat, but because of my own native yearning. This was a giant step toward seeing more. Across the country our elders were battling the shades that shrank our minds and abbreviated our world. We thought the corner was cool, but more than that we deeply believed that we could do no better, that this tiny parcel was all we deserved in this world of sin.

I was exposed at Lemmel. To be a black male is to be always at war, and no flight to the county can save us, because even there we are met by the assumption of violence, by the specter of who we might turn on next. I was ravaged by the plague of my fallen old town and reengineered. They took my wings, handed me a blade. I lost so much of myself out there. My dreams shrank into survival and mere dignity and respect. But in my djembe, I found art and my lost imagination, and now from heavy hands to making a drum sing—what more was out there? How far did it all really go?

That year, the Mecca sent me a letter. Kelly had graduated. Kris was still there. Bill was hanging on. I had long ago given up, and though I now felt I might actually become something, I was resigned that the Mecca was out of reach. But the old temple was hurting. Children of the integrated class were now gunning for white people's ice. I had done well enough on my PSAT to attract their attention, which apparently did not extend to my grades. They invited our family to a dinner, along with a pool of other black potentials. I walked into a ballroom filled with round tables and black kids seated with their parents. They served us three courses and the usual parade of speakers vouching for the great esteem of the Mecca. The university president stood last, and his were the only words that stuck with me. His topic was the ubiquity of Howard across everything from dentistry to architecture to education. Anywhere you go in the world, he told us, you can find one of us.

Afterward in the car, my parents asked what I thought. It was okay, I guess. It didn't seem all that. Truth was, I was covering. I was convinced that my high school career was so marred that I'd never really be considered for admission. So I covered with apathy. Dad went ballistic—

Boy, this is an opportunity, and the best you can do is sit back there and mumble and shrug your shoulders?

I should have taken heart from Big Bill, who through it all had found his way in. Of course, he was now alone. He stopped checking in with Dad, though Dad lessons and words were now working harder on him. He'd come to Howard with cartoon ideas to gird him against failure. Only the weak, with their fucked-up jump shots, off-brand kicks, and feeble arms could thrive in class. That was his defense, because he was sure that he could not make it himself. But now broke, flunking, and on the verge of an escort back home, he confronted the truth. There were brothers here like him, paladins of the streets, who swore to the same codes, and yet they were getting over. What would be his defense now?

He still could not see the merits of scholarship, independent of all else. But he loved the life, the parties, the herb sessions, the controlled independence, and the waves of Jennifers for as far as he could see. He could go back home and invest in his old ties. He could work in the district and spend his lunches and off days with an empty book bag, perpetrating on the yard. But inside, he was not a half stepper. If it was going to be school, then it would be all the way. It was time to play his part.

The transition did not come easy—he never learned to sit down for hours every night with his head in a book. But he started showing up for class, and found that he liked the methodology, the back and forth of debates. He partied less, cut off old friends, and mastered the great art of the cram. Slowly it came together, and at the end of his first semester of any effort, he saw what he could do—a C plus GPA—if he only tried.

Dad was ecstatic, and for the first time he got some idea that all his labor might not be washed away.

I took my last SAT in November of my senior year, and what I remembered most was that it meant an exit from the prep classes taught by Jovett and my mom. Kier was out of Poly, too, and began hanging with new friends near Barrington. It was no longer the island I remembered, for not even the great cloud giants could keep the rotting city at bay. Kier ran into Barrington's collapse, and whereas I was unsure of what I wanted and how I would get there, Kier was on intimate terms with his own desires. He wanted a mass of ends, accessible by a shortcut, and so he turned to the drug trade.

We parted ways there. I was too formed by then, and firm in my own ethics and beliefs of what crack had done to us all, clawing out the eyes of our cities with its steel-white talons. At school, I cut off Ebony at every pass. We talked almost every night for hours about all the nothing that young people feel the fate of worlds hinges on. After school, we'd hang out at the library or the sub shop across the street. I gathered her life story, how she was originally from Jersey, and how drugs had taken both her parents down. She moved in with a godmother out in the county and came to high school away from all the problems of the city. Of course, by then Woodlawn was also shifting over. In ten years, the neighborhood mall would go from the Gap, arcades, and Hecht's to check-cashing joints, fast-food, and plus-size clothing stores.

On the surface of it all, she was unbroken and serene. Once, she challenged my father to a debate over his revolutionary credentials—made him justify a Black Panther who'd moved to the suburbs. He was forty-six, and was moving toward a lighter touch with my younger brother, Menelik. He did not preach much now, as he was entering into the twilight of his parenting years. My mother might go away for a weekend, and Dad would cook, wash dishes, and take us to the movies. He walked in on us studying, wearing reading glasses, pulled low on his nose. He looked down at us sitting at the table and then pulled up a seat. She grinned immediately, and then grilled him on the ethics of talking black while leaving the least among us behind. It was good and spirited, and Dad's logic was indomitable as usual. Still, it didn't stop Ebony from asserting my claims to the West Side were little more than fraud.

Beneath it all, I saw her wounds, the thing that makes men run into burning houses. Here was my damsel. All her demons were hidden, but I could feel them baying out from within and activating something immutable in my DNA. My grades improved in direct proportion to the time I spent around her. I got extracurricular. I did a Garvey speech for the school in the black awareness assembly. I became a peer counselor. They'd pull me out of class for workshops on conflict resolution.

My motives were impure, like my brother's: Ebony was involved in all of these things. She was one of those kids. She caught me in the hallway after sixth period. She'd been gone all day and was wearing a dress that seemed like it was bought for church. She'd just been honored for grades, for extraordinary effort or some such accolade of overachieving. She was always overachieving. She handed me an envelope and told me not to open it until after school.

I had to go to Mondawmin that day for shopping, and thought little of what I'd mindlessly stuffed in my backpack. I opened it after I got off the subway. It was the program from her ceremony, and on the side was a love note that I could not recognize as such. It was written in that vague, noncommittal way of a girl who wants you to know what she feels but wants to protect herself all the same. I did not know what I was holding, and was caught on the price in self-esteem for figuring it out. I talked to her that night and thanked her, but I did not push like I was supposed to. I could not see that beneath the shield, beneath the smiles and laughter that were her armor, behind the glowing ax, all of us are waiting to be swept away.

My mother extended her SAT classes for the kids at Sankofa. I would come downstairs on Sunday mornings and make faces at them before I headed out. I was looking out the window into manhood and independence. No one hassled me about my grades. No one checked on me in my room. My parents went out of town and left me with now nine-year-old Menelik. I took him to his Little League football games. That was a great season, the first time in my life where I'd been turned loose from the parental vise grip. Still, you could not dent the expectations of my mother. She would bring me college catalogs. Dad took me down to the civic center for the historically black college tour. I imagined myself in Tougaloo, Tennessee State, Dillard, or Johnson C. Smith, somewhere else with a different way of living and perhaps the sort of standards that would admit a screwup like me.

At school, I caught the attention of teachers and counselors who tried to move me into Advanced Placement. I politely declined, no need to soil my last year. Still, in spite of me, some of them managed to place road signs in my life path. My English 12 teacher, Mrs. Effron, saw my papers and short stories and was the first person, outside of my mother, to tell me that in this I may have a gift. My guidance counselor, Mr. Herring, took to me immediately and put out of his mind my earlier transcript and three years of ineptitude. When the applications began to fly, he wrote me a recommendation that was beyond anything I felt I had earned. I saw in myself the disgrace to my father's name. But Mr. Herring was a black man, Conscious like my father, and thus desperate to reclaim troops for the field.

That winter, I applied to four schools—all in the area, in hopes of never saying good-bye to my drummers. The shortest application was for Howard—a gamble, a pebble slung into the dark. Then I returned to the last leisurely half of senior year. That was the year, the only year of my childhood, that I took off from hip-hop. The older gods were falling off. EPMD were breaking. Chuck and Flav had taken us as far as they could, and already the new voices were being hijacked by the death cults. Brothers who last week were shouting out Malcolm were flipped into studio gangsters, killing every nigger in sight. I felt some part of that need to stand on the corner of the world and grab your nuts. But I was at the gates of manhood, and they could not fade me. They were hard where it mattered least—attacking whole genders, claiming to run the street, and then fleeing in the wake of the Beast.

By then, Big Bill had brought home other gifts—Bob, Steel Pulse, and Burning Spear. He would gather his friends at our home, my parents gone for the week, and blaze out back, banging *Babylon by Bus*. They were all nouveau Conscious, had dropped their slave names for handles taken from Zulu and Swahili. Bob Marley had been dead for a decade, and yet he emerged to us as the great bard of our people. Later I found the frat boys had ruined him, like they do everything they touch. But back then, he was prophetic. That year I did not know where I was headed, but I knew that I was mortgaged to the grand ideal—the end of mental slavery and the fulfillment of the book.

In those last lazy months of senior year—half days and free periods—I was admitted to Morgan State, sent a dorm room assignment and glossy package extolling my new independent life. It was my third acceptance, all to local schools, and all the product of three quarters of grinding from a 1.8 to a respectable 2.4 grade point.

Who was I in those moments of acceptance but a boy finally realized? All my years my family pounded me in hopes of something more. My mother told me I was sharp, but would never make it this lazy. My father could drown a whole weekend into chores. Big Bill would punch me in the arm, warning that out there was a world out of control and the safeties were permanently disengaged. My mother used to say I was going to fly, but I could not see how. And now I'd come home and in the mailbox, each month, I found a fat packet with my name on it. I was not made complete, but I felt worthy of my mother's praise.

I didn't show for graduation. I took on my father's aversion for ceremony, and had only a year of ties to Wood-lawn. I dismissed senior prom from the day I came to Woodlawn. The year would be a trip of unfortunate busi-ness—there was no time for flowers. But then this girl Ebony, and this silly compulsion within, clouded my logic and I could not see. Plus, as always, I missed the intricate signs, the hints, and head fakes, the looks when I was not looking. I did the math too late, and by then she'd taken up with another dude. Man, listen, he was straight Christo-pher Williams, the sort of pretty boy who pulled strictly redbones, until he heard Mike G, got on that blacker-the-berry shit, and came to the other side. Of course, I wasn't that far off, but when I saw them walking the halls, it felt wrong as Winnie and Kirk McCray.

I stopped calling after that. What did it matter—I was on my way, stepping out of the world and into my next self. My mother demanded proof, suspected another scheme ending in the repetition of the twelfth grade. She knew her child, and in some way could not believe that the saga was coming to an end. Until I brought the diploma home from the principal's office, opened the hardcover vinyl folder, and placed it in her hands, she did not believe. When she saw it, she just half smiled, no big hug, no inspiring speech, just happy to see the end.

I had the vague sense that something different was afoot. Dad ambushed me in the brown Honda Accord, our third one, because Ma had crashed up the other two. We were driving from the new office. Dad turned down Wabash, pulled into a tiny shopping mall, and parked in front of Kmart. Dad owed me nothing, except fatherhood and that was how he always carried it. My father never apologized for one minute of parenting. He didn't start there in that parking lot, and yet he talked in a manner that was less sure.

Son, he told me. I have begun another relationship. I am in a relationship with Jovett. Me and your mother thought you should know. I love Jovett and your mother very much. We all thought you should know.

He asked if I had questions, how I felt, what I needed to say. I have never expressed anger with my father, to my father. Fear clouded every word. But here was an open shot. I could have yelled, stepped out of the car, slammed the door. I could have run away for a week, told him I hated him like white kids I'd seen in movies. Here was the chink in his armor, the flaw which had always been theory finally confirmed. Even the general falls down, though it must be said, fallen is not how he saw himself at the time. Still, I did nothing. I said nothing, just nodded my head and listened until it was time to drive away.

CHAPTER 8

Use your condom,
take sips of the brew

When I was young, my father was heroic to me, was all I
knew of religion. His word was the difference between pancakes and oatmeal, between Speed Racer and yard work.
Every trip to the Food Barn was epic. We'd hop out of the
car, and I'd try to shut the door in rhythm with him, like on
detective shows when they meant business. He was heroic
because I was a child, because my worldview didn't extend
past Lode Runner, Train 9, or Warren Moon's rookie card.

The first time Dad beat me, I was six and the subject of my first-grade teacher's phone calls home. In those days, all the kids anyone cared about got beatings. But that black leather belt, folded on my parents' bed was still terrible, and this was my clearest illustration that fatherhood was dictatorship, that its subjects were at the mercy of a tyrannical God.

By the time I hit Lemmel, my appraisal of Dad depended on the year, how I woke up, the number of hours I'd worked in the basement. There were days I would have wished him into nothing, so that I could be free to relish in dumb shit with all the other laughing, orphaned boys. There were others, when I looked around and saw that, though the birthright of every child was a manned fortress, we lived in unnatural times. All the guardians had fled their posts, and here was mine, his hand on his sword, his armor glimmering in the light of moons. Now he sat in his car, across from me, unveiling his true face, unveiling a tangled humanity that made all my foibles look elementary.

In his mind he was righteous, and still wedded to the old Panther idea of free, unbound love. He did not speak to me in shame so much as struggled to display himself to a child. But Dad was obsessed with the world as he thought it should be, and his ideals were a bright light, blinding him even to his beloved. So the losses my family took were not spoken, and, as we rejected Christmas, Thanksgiving, and the Fourth, we were swaddled in a great cloak of alone. Even the most mundane act—refusing the Pledge of Allegiance, sitting mute for the flag—pushed us farther down the path of resistance and alienation from the rest of the world. He didn't acknowledge this truth because the superseding truth was that he was right about it. He wouldn't bend to the will of a backward world and wouldn't allow us not to bend either. I was sure that everyone else my age was frolicking in pagan October masks, eating hamburgers and pie à la mode, backstroking through a lake of Christmas presents, while I meditated among stacks of tofu and books. Even after I got Conscious, I felt I'd been robbed of time, that I had been isolated from a series of great childhood events. In my father's house, values ripped us from the crowd. Dad called it enlightenment. But to me it just felt lonely.

My mother had fallen out of step with the world she once knew and looked sideways at her family's everyday values. Even without my father, she would have been a dissident, cracking wise in the corner at reunions. But Dad could not come to even that sort of détente. And so with each new revelation he laid upon our family—no meat, no

Thanksgiving—she grew further apart from her peoples. Once we drove to Columbia for a family portrait with all my maternal uncles, aunts, and cousins. My grandmother stood in the back, proud matriarch who'd battled her way up from Gilmore Homes. The photographer was gregarious and white and late. I could feel the sharp edges of Dad's painted smile.

Afterward, everyone went for dinner, everyone except us. I had cousins who'd been off to Germany, who I hadn't seen in years, but I just climbed into the car, sulked in the back, and looked out the window at the highway dark. We were halfway home. Dad was frustrated because the photographer had been late. And then he popped—

Son, do you know how many black photographers there are in Baltimore, struggling? Why am I driving all the way to Columbia to help out the other man? I'm sorry, Son. They've gotten enough of my money for one night.

His logic cut through my anger, and the sense of it left me reeling for weeks. But I still just wanted him to let it go, if only for that evening.

This was how my mother was walled off from everything, her own past, her family, choices about her present. Every bold idea took us further out. From our very names, my mother had so much to explain to the world—and now this—a man out of pocket, with his woman's insane blessing. She buckled in shame, and the thought of explaining this one, of going out into the world smiling and claiming the high ground, was too much.

She knew that this was the reality for so many women, but she was robbed of even the cover of fake ignorance. She was ashamed, and the fact that things were not public was little help. You must know that my mother was hard as hell, would beat children like a street fight, and then drill us on long division. But Ma was of her time and that giant sect of black women, who, rendered fatherless, would have gone barren before staging a repeat.

For the gift of having a father around for her children, something the rest of this thieving country took as natural as rain, so much else suffered. There was never music playing when my peoples walked into the living room. You could not catch them on old choppy home videos, making out under a summer tree, laughing, holding up their protesting hands as the lenses closed in. They were not for the smoky jazz clubs, dinner reservations, or walks down at the harbor. They barely marked anniversaries. As for me and that time, there were the facts my mother laid down to me from the day I could talk—that people were people and their covenants were sealed with subterfuge, conspiracy, and denial. When my father opened his marriage, when he explained this new joining in that brown Honda Accord, it was just another bizarre step in our bizarre lives. It was how I was raised. It was what I'd come to expect.

I never talked to Kier about any of this, though I was told that he'd been informed. What I saw of him and my father continued as normal—Dad would hand him parables from *Up from Slavery*, or Kier would perfect his imitation of Dad's '70s cadence. By then, Kier had chosen the glittering path. I always thought he had what mattered— the cool hand, the fresh Ewings, Champion hoodie, the badass dimes. Yet he craved frenzy, life on the random and quick. Like all boys, I saw the appeal. I would not live on lucky numbers but a long blessed grind. I thought Kier labored in the shadow of his father's death, and even today I'm not sure that Dad helped. By the time that last summer came, the footprints we left were hardening in the sun.

But soon I'd be loose from it all, and I felt the freedom of eighteen on the approach. I was a high-school senior, with an assigned dorm room. Everything in front of me was green sky.

All year, I'd been working toward better drumming, showing up early for classes, teaching young children, and tinkering with the threading and tightness of my own djembe. I bought a third drum, decked out with carvings of the Continent, a brown stain, and a polyurethane glow. By March, even my breath was a djembe beat, and everything revolved around my next rehearsal, drum class, or show. In the meantime, Sankofa was prepping for our biggest concert of the year, the spring recital.

The spring recital was always a coming out—we wore different sets of costumes, tied fabric around our heads, or wore leather helmets with straw spiking out like Mohawks. Dancers and drummers spanned all the ages, from five to seventy-five. This year was bigger, because demand had grown so much that two concerts had been scheduled on two different nights. At the last spring recital, I was young with this, and when they called me out to solo during drum call, all I could do was amble to the middle of the stage, bend slightly forward, and murmur something that got some polite applause but didn't rupture time and space. Now my hands had been cleaned by practice in the breezeway, shaving goatskins in the basement, and the simple rigors of repetition.

Spring recital came on the week of my driver's ed classes, and as much as I loved drumming, driving was too old a fantasy to sacrifice for Sankofa rehearsals. The dream crystallized back in middle school. One day I spotted Big Bill's homeboy Anthony while I was standing on Garrison waiting for the number 91. Anthony was an MC in my brother's high-school collective, nasty with the lyrics, the sort of odd, quiet kid who sits off in the corner, nodding his head, then grabs a mic and unveils the Cain Marko. Whenever I saw him, I heard his signature couplet—"So they'll read in the morning with papers delivered / Another whack rapper found dead in the river."

Anthony's parents had sprung for a neon-green Jeep with a brown retractable hood, which he later crashed. I was enamored when he offered me a ride, and noted how his system shook the roof and, more than usual, robbed our small talk of any real point. The whip made him limitless. He could have driven to Old Crow and never looked back. From then on, in my feature dreams, I cruised down Garrison pumping Maxi Priest and Shabba, unleashing the base, until I caught the eye of an original Spinderella, Isis, or Terrible T, her tennis skirt fluttering over matching slouch socks, all-white Classics, or pink Air Force Ones.

For driver's ed, I missed almost every drumming rehearsal that week, which tore my heart and left me mourning in the back of class, while my instructor went off on rights of way, the exact distances from curbs, stop signs, fire hydrants, the weight of a cop's hand versus red lights. I just placed my palms on my thighs in ready position, leaned back in my wooden chair until I was five hundred years away, until I stood in the court of Mansa Musa, in a kufi and a dark robe. My djembe hung from my shoulders, and when the Lion of Mali nodded, my hands fired and called across the Sahel. The teacher would lower the lights and show films on driver safety. But I would play lead on my lap, imagining dancers who kicked and leaped through the dark like great black flamingoes.

That whole week I felt sidelined and disarmed. I didn't think about Ebony, pretty boy, or the prom. I didn't think about my dorm room awaiting me at Morgan or Ma lobbying the Mecca for my admission. In the back of class, I traced my fingers like maps. Back on Tioga they had teased me, said I had the hands of a very glamorous blonde. But now my palms were Himalayas. Callous skin shielded my joints. I was harder now. I could play the traditional rhythm for the dance, Lamba, for hours, just me, a lead, and a djun-djun. I could sit in my father's basement armed with rope, goatskin, and wood, and yank and pull until spirits said my name.

On Friday, our last day, they gave us a driving test so easy that even I, with all my day-tripping, managed to ace. Ma scooped me up and headed straight for the studio on Eager Street. At yellow lights I exhorted her on—Go, go, go. She laughed and looked cockeyed—Boy, you gonna cause an accident. She dropped me off at the door and I dashed up the staircase in doubles, and now I could hear the drums roaring, and young sisters singing in tongues that they did not understand. But that was always irrelevant. The whole point was to reach beyond the coherent and touch what we were, what we lost, when the jackboots of history pinned us down.

The drumming was so loud when I entered the studio that when the mamas and babas smiled and greeted—they always smiled for me—I could only see them mouthing above the din. The brothers were working the prelude to Mandiani, which is slow like the gathering of warning clouds. Salim, the youthful master, was playing my drum, which normally was nothing, but I was in the mode of a full fiend and had just put on a new slamming off-white skin with a few black freckles. He saw me and stood up and offered me a space and the lead. I sat down and promptly went out of my head. I snowballed high above everything and drove the pace like a warhorse pushed into pursuit.

By the time the sisters got to solos, I'd sweated through my red Sankofa tee. I was standing, my djembe suspended from my waist by my long white strap. They were all lined up, banging their feet in rhythm against the wooden dance floor. They extended their hands like pharaohs, waiting for me to summon them one at a time with a break. But I showed off first, because what Sankofa taught me was that deep down, I loved the crowd, that after days of Dad's isolationism, I simply could not get enough of the people. I wish I could remember the order in which I brought the dancers out. It must have been by age.

It's all now a blur of images—Milcah's attitude, me playing slaps and pointing to the floor; Elishibah's hands reap-
ing the air, her long dreads pulled back on her head and
spraying out like a crown of snakes. I know Menes was off
somewhere and Salim finished us all up, and afterward we
laughed and gave dap.

That whole summer I felt on. It wasn't just the annual
concert—it was AFRAM, Artscape, the random events at
community centers, weddings in mosques, to which we
were invited to bring our drums. The crowds lost their balance when the djembe hit. Sisters would dance in the aisles.
Mamas from other companies would jump on stage. Fat
women in tight denim would leap up and move with power
and grace. Teen dancers would rush out before their cue.
Mama Kibibi could not hold them back. And then there
were the faces of my family when I came out to solo—Big
Bill, clapping and pumping his fist before adding a few
bucks to the pile of money at the front of the stage. Sometimes I'd look out and spot my father, nodding with his eyes
closed, letting the drums roar over him.

I could have stayed like that forever, drumming my
way in and out of various corners of Baltimore. I did not
know where it led, but I would have slept on heat grates,
worn scraps and overalls, shaken my cup down on Charles

Street, and dined in the basements of churches, if I could have just left things as they were. My talent was second tier and I knew I would always be a workman, a support player for someone else's glorious show. But I was so in love, and so of the spirit, that I just did not care.

I got Ebony down to class at Sankofa during that summer. She tried dancing, and afterward I cracked jokes because she could barely tie her lappa, because she was behind the beat. She just smiled and jabbed at my arm. Afterward, we'd head down to the harbor to the movies, then out to Burger King and debate *Boyz in the Hood* versus *Menace*. Still, we were teenagers, and so always closest on the phone. I apologized late one night, told her I should have taken her hand, that I should have been stronger in what I saw and felt. But we were both the best we could have been. At that age, the deep attractions, the ones that threaten your open future, may thrill you, may kidnap your days, but more powerful is the flood of terror, the nakedness you feel when she only starts walking your way.

The heat rolled in around June, and with it visions of my actual future. I awoke at dawn and saw my mother out back, turned south toward Mecca in prayer, then grinding rabbit bones, collecting herbs, muttering incantations. Even through expulsions, fights, and idleness, she had not lost faith in a voyage to Howard. What I could not understand was that she believed that I was owed, that no matter what

216

I'd done in high school, somehow, I was entitled to see the Mecca, to find my place in the great black cosmopolis. My parents were two-faced. To me, they showed no mercy. They preached from the Book of Fallen Children—Commandment 1: The Child Is Always Ungrateful. At eighteen, the free ride would stop, and I'd be dumped into the mess of the world. But in their private moments, they were soft, cowed by love. They critiqued their own parenting skills and thought of all the ways they could help their kids get ahead.

She was still working in D.C., and weekly she would appear, unannounced, in the admissions office and demand a status report. That June, Howard sent notice that they wanted to see my final grades and another letter of recommendation. Ma felt the walls weakening and continued her assault—morning prayer, regular visits where she dropped Dad's name and those of the three kids who had, by now, either graduated or were still on campus.

The fat packet struck, like LT from the blind side. There I am, having the summer of my life, and then this day I walk up Campfield hill, my bagged drum strapped to my back, and checking the mail, see this envelope long and heavy and when turned over note that it bears the seal of the Mecca. By Gabriel Prosser's ghost, I thought. This is it.

I ripped it open before I made it in the front door, and did not even have need for the acceptance letters. They don't send brochures and leaflets to rejects. When Ma came home, I showed her the packet and she laughed in that loud, joyous, voluminous way that is the signature of all her proper sisters. She would have leaped and pumped her fist, if that was how she got down. This was her acceptance, after all. What had I done my whole life but obstructed my own way out?

Back when I first got Conscious, the Mecca seemed natural, the only place to bring me into line with spirit of the El-Hajj Shabazz. But with each failing year, I lowered myself, once to the point that I didn't even think a college would take me. True, the Mecca was only an hour away, and there were drummers in Chocolate City. But the bond I felt here was more than music: it was an enveloping community, a circle so tight that it reverberated in me even when I was gone for days. What I knew even then was that I would never be in love like that again, was that nothing that healthy would ever feel that carnal, lush, and complete.

I'm going to Morgan, I told my parents. They were sitting down in my father's office. My mother gave a speech about opportunity and responsibility. Dad sat back, with his patented face of stone and just listened to me and Ma go back and forth. At the end, he placed his palms on his lap and said, Son, it's your choice. You're grown. You can make up your mind.

I walked out of the office with a fool's smile. How I ever thought I'd prevailed, how I ever thought that I would win against my mother is beyond me now. I had turned it around, but not so much that I was scholarship worthy—my parents would still be carrying the bill. And I was in the burgeoning class of kids whose families made too much for financial aid but not enough to make tuition payments anything less than a war.

We had two more conversations. In the first, Dad continued the charade of options. Son, it's still your choice. But your mother is my woman, and, Son, she has power. I think she's right, but you're grown and can make your own decision. I am trying to let you know that. But your mother, Son. Your mother has power.

I want to go to Morgan, I told him.

Okay, Son.

But by the next week, he was flipped. We were in his office again. My mother had that thin smile like You Know What This Is. The conversation was short.

Dad: Ta-Nehisi. You're not going to thirteenth grade.

And like that, it was done. All over again, I was exiled from home and destined for Mecca.

Or this is what I saw. Fact was, I was only months from eighteen, and could have done what I wanted. I was split on leaving Baltimore, and the wishes of my parents were an easy out. I did not know then that this is what life is—just when you master the geometry of one world, it slips away, and suddenly again, you're swarmed by strange shapes and impossible angles.

But I had survived my formative world and all its trappings. Down on Tioga, the reports of my old friends floated back to me. Their fates were maddeningly clichéd. Even the ones in whom I saw a tighter head game fell into shadow, became a statistic in the cold hands of some pundit, who looked out on our streets and rolled up his windows. I still walked under a cloak of doubt. I could wake up one morning like—Time to start the revolution, or I could wind up in rags, sleeping on heating grates, permanently retired to the dreamworlds that I'd conjured since childhood.

I spent my last week closing it all out. I played a final set with my Sankofa brothers. We argued because the sound wasn't tight. We said that it wasn't the end, that I was merely a weekend commuter train away. But already, I felt the distance. I said good-bye to Ebony the way we did everything important—over the phone. I took one of the teen dancers to see some smooth jazz. Another girl from my

Poly days visited the night before I left. The weathermen were predicting a meteor shower behind heavy cloud cover, and when we looked up we could see the sky flashing like lightning in a thunderless storm. She must have handed me a gift. We talked for an hour or so on my back porch, then she rose, gave me a hug, and pulled off in a blue minivan.

The next morning, I brought boxes and suitcases to the front door. Jovett and my parents were seated at the dining room table. On the table were various gifts from Jovett—a set of screwdrivers, a fire extinguisher, a flashlight, several packs of rubbers. Dad would not have loaded up that car without a lecture, but what he said, I can't even remember. I was caught between competing things—the bliss of leaving the dominion of my father and the sorrow of the impending loss of my brothers.

We pulled off, drove down Campfield hill, up Liberty Road, to the Beltway, and down 95, until we reached the new world. We found Big Bill right off Georgia Avenue, sitting on the shallow wall in front the Howard Plaza Towers—where he had once let off, sprayed the night sky with a gun—which was now my home. He was sitting with two of his friends, in a fisherman's cap, khaki shorts, white tee shirt, Timbs. He had never looked so at ease. He was sitting there talking when we pulled up, loose with the sort of casual humanity that Baltimore never allowed. The old anger, which guarded him and maybe saved him during the days of Murphy Homes, was drained and what was left was all my father, all my people, ever wanted. Was a man.

When I took hajj at the Mecca, my parents didn't open an ancient bottle of wine. They didn't take any vacations. I was not the last child but the last of that perilous bunch, the sixth in seven years, born into lust, a frenzy of variables, and many futures tossed in the air. Now, for the first time in almost twenty years, there was space to reflect. Who would they be now that the great labors lay behind them? Now that they'd shielded the kids from the era of crack?

There was still my young brother, Menelik. But the air and water just weren't the same. He had a Sega Genesis. He went to Fallstaff. His only vice was Gundam Wing. He was not a wanderer or insurgent but was balanced, had a sort of everyday aesthetic that I'd always wanted. He was mostly quiet, and on the weekends would go see foreign flicks with my father. He barely remembered Tioga; and Campfield, the sort of Avalon I prayed for back at Lemmel, was his formative home.

For him, for everyone, the old rules were falling away. A month before I left, Sankofa had a cookout in a small park in Woodlawn, to celebrate the Fourth of July. It was my father's birthday, but we'd never celebrated the date. Babas and mamas brought out potato salad, grilled turkey burgers, and veggie dogs. That was the summer, when Super Soakers were wild. I had never owned so much as a water gun, because in our time, so many kids were falling that such toys were a mark of the enslaved 85. But that whole afternoon gunfights broke out. Some fool strapped two tanks to his back and started spraying like Blowtorch. I grabbed someone else's double barrel and went to work. Amid the crossfire, the whole cookout laughing and wet, I saw my brother, small and shirtless, clutching a baby water pistol with an orange neon tank on the top. Menelik ran through the streams of water, until he found himself in the clear. Then he raised the iron at an oblivious target, smiled, and fired.

ACKNOWLEDGMENTS

The acknowledgments begin with the love of my life, Kenyatta Matthews, without whom this book simply could not have been. There is no other way to say that. I thank my mother (Ma, you're only second cause you got the dedication), who used to make me write essays whenever I got into trouble, explaining exactly what I'd done and why I'd done it. This book begins with her, to whom I am, obviously, immeasurably indebted. Love to my grandmother Anna Waters. Love to my aunt Ava and my aunt JoAnn. Love to my cousins Jeff, Kevin, and Jo-Jo.

A shout-out to my father, Paul Coates, who, when I was thirteen, handed me a copy of Greg Tate's *Flyboy in the Buttermilk*. I didn't know what the hell Greg was talking about. But I knew that somewhere in the world there were people whose life work it was to play with language and unpack the diction of Chuck D. That was all I needed to know. Peace to Greg Tate, for that initial spark.

Peace to my brother Damani, who introduced me to hip-hop and poetry, thus seeding the initial thoughts for this book. Peace to my brother John, who helped subsidize this endeavor in the last months. Peace to Malik, who guided me through *Keep on the Borderlands, Against the Giants,* and *Castle Amber.* Those days still walk with me, all the way through this book. Peace to my sisters, Kris and Kelly, for constant encouragement. Peace to Menelik, and congratulations on doing me one better and actually making it out of Mecca. Peace to those coming up next to bat—Tye, N'namdi, Christian, Samori, Christopher, Oronde, Marley. Love to you all.

Peace to anyone who ever, at any point, worked for *Washington City Paper,* an institution that changed my life. Thanks to David Carr, who hired me off of some middling college newspaper columns. Thanks to Bradford Mckee, one of the greatest editors I've ever worked with. Thanks to the great friends I met there: Amanda Ripley, Michael Schaffer, Stephanie Mencimer (who shepherded me through the *Washington Monthly* in lean times), Eric Wemple, Caroline Schweiter, Sean Daly, John Cloud, Jason Cherkis, Amy Austin. Please forgive me if I missed anyone. I'm getting old. Love to all of you. Those were some of the best times of my life.

Thanks to my agent Gloria Loomis. Thanks to Walter Mosley for the opportunity. Thanks to my editor Christopher Jackson, who cultivated this idea from small-talk over lunch to an actual book. Thanks to everyone at Spiegel & Grau—Mya Spalter, Meghan Walker, Lucy Silag, Cindy Spiegel, and Julie Grau. Thanks to any editor who ever took a chance on me. Thanks to Bill Saporito, Nathan Thornburgh, and Lisa Cullen, without whom my stay at *Time* would likely have been shorter. Thanks to Paul Tough and Ilena Silverman, both of whom gave me huge breaks.

Props to Jelani Cobb, Joel Dias-Porter, Brian Gilmore, Natalie Hopkinson, Natalie Moore, Kenneth Carroll, and Bridget Warren. Every one of you is/was instrumental in my education. Props to my man Ben Talton, who always believed, and his wife, Janai Nelson, still my favorite debating partner. Props to my good friends Neil Drumming, Dawnie Walton, and Ricardo Gutierrez, who've listened to me drone on about this book for too long. Props to Brendan Koerner and Eyal Press, perhaps the two biggest reasons I haven't tossed out my laptop and enrolled in culinary school. Props to Colby Poulson and GS. I shall see you all in the battlegrounds again, one way or another.